AMERICA:
THE FINAL CHAPTER

Also by Jessi Winchester

From Bordello to Ballot Box

AMERICA:
THE FINAL CHAPTER

JESSI WINCHESTER

Trafford Publishing
Indianapolis, Indiana

Printed in Victoria, BC, Canada.

ISBN: 978-1-4269-1991-6 (sc)
ISBN: 978-1-4269-1992-3 (dj)

Library of Congress Control Number: 2009939890

*Our mission is to efficiently provide the world's finest, most comprehensive book publishing
service, enabling every author to experience success. To find out how to publish your book, your
way, and have it available worldwide, visit us online at www.trafford.com*

Trafford rev. 11/19/2009

 www.trafford.com

North America & international
toll-free: 1 888 232 4444 (USA & Canada)
phone: 250 383 6864 ♦ fax: 812 355 4082

For my grandson Cody Schwarz, a proud Marine - and for every extraordinary man and woman in uniform - especially our Wounded Warriors and those who made the ultimate sacrifice on behalf of freedom.

Contents

PART THREE

"Whoever wishes to foresee the future must consult the past; for human events ever resemble those of preceding times."

~Machiavelli; 1469-1527
Italian Political Philosopher

PART ONE

Chapter 1

WARNINGS FROM HISTORY

"Those who do not learn from the past, are destined to repeat it."
~ George Santayana 1863-1952
"Reason in Common Sense" Novelist

Historians throughout the ages have tried to impress the importance of learning the lessons from past historical cycles but humans, being what they are, simply continue to let the wise words of those learned men fall on deaf ears. America is at a critical moment in its democratic evolution. The election of 2008 was perhaps the most important election in the history of the nation and the direction President Barack Obama takes will determine if democracy continues in America or if it goes the way of other declining nations.

The road map history provides has been validated by over 2,000 years of predictable rise-and-fall cycles of history's great nations. Only if we study and learn from the past in an effort to make wise decisions for the present, will America prevent itself from repeating disastrous history in the future.

Scottish historian Alexander Tyler studied some of the most powerful republics in history and found a recurring sequence, which should give modern day America great pause. He noted that a democracy *"will continue to exist up until the time that voters discover they can vote themselves generous gifts from the public treasury and from that moment on, the majority always votes for the candidates who promise the most benefits from the public treasury. The result is that every democracy will finally collapse due to loose fiscal policy, which is always followed by a dictatorship."* The progression has predictable steps from oppression (England's rule in the case of America) to courage (Revolutionary War), to liberty (Declaration of Independence), to abundance, to complacency, to apathy, to dependence on a central governing body, back into oppression.

As America's very first president, George Washington forged an unknown path within the Office of the President. He had no precedent or outline other than the newly minted Constitution of the United States, which put him in good stead for designing the standards of the office and the person entrusted to that extraordinary position. The nation's first president took an oath that above all else, the president would follow the law of the land, the U.S. Constitution, and do what was best for the people of the fledgling country. He set an amazing example for presidents to follow in the future – if only they would.

After fighting for America's independence from England, George Washington guided the nation along the heady road of democracy. The U.S. Constitution was his instruction manual and he followed its laws with reverence. Since that time the nation has had good, bad, and mediocre presidents whose administrations have taken the nation up and down hills and valleys. As time progressed some even changed how the Founders intended the nation to be run and administrations began to pull farther and father away from the nation's blueprint, the U.S. Constitution.

The Declaration of Independence, the Bill of Rights, and the United States Constitution set forth the direction and principles the Founders intended for the nation. Some delegates such as George Mason saw the larger picture and refused to sign the Declaration of Independence because he had the ability to see far into the future and recognized the Founders had not put enough safeguards in place in the documents to prevent the abuses that ultimately surfaced in future administrations. Until Andrew Jackson's term the vision set forth for the nation was upheld but it began an administration-by-administration decline from Jackson's time forward.

Andrew Jackson was one of the earliest presidents to circumvent the basic tenets of the Declaration of Independence and break the law. In 1823 the U.S. Supreme Court declared Native Americans had the right to live on their tribal land in Georgia but the state and federal governments wanted the gold on their land so they were determined to eradicate them. To that end, the Indian Removal Act was passed by Congress in 1830 at which time Jackson defiantly declared, *"The Supreme Court made their decision; now let them enforce it."* Ignoring the Supreme Court ruling, he unlawfully and forcefully removed American Indians from their tribal land. Defying the Declaration of Independence didn't seem to bother him any more than ignoring court decisions.

The colonies' battle for independence from England's oppression was still fresh in the minds of the new country's residents so determining they were no better off under the new form of government, they concluded their lives would be better if they broke away from the Union and ruled themselves. Language in the Declaration of Independence grants states the right to secede and South Carolina made clear their intent, yet Jackson sent armed troops to force them to remain in the Union, thereby ignoring a basic right of a state and propelling the nation down a side path away from the guidelines of the Founders and the laws of the land. From his administration forward, most succeeding presidencies moved yet a little farther from the intent of the Constitution.

Abraham Lincoln carried the path away from the Constitution even farther when he virtually changed the power structure of the country from a states' rights nation to a centralized government. He ignored and circumvented the Tenth Amendment of the Bill of Rights, which limits federal power and grants states all powers not given to the federal government by the U.S. Constitution and instead declared the primary power belonged to the federal government rather than the people as the Bill of Rights intended. By so doing, he conferred powers to himself as president that were not bestowed by Founding documents or in the best interest of the nation.

Woodrow Wilson intentionally sought the advise of a socialist and implemented illegal and immoral actions against the people he took an oath to protect. The Oath of Office is crystal clear about swearing a president to, *"preserve, protect and defend the Constitution of the United States,"* yet Wilson willfully ignored that pledge.

Franklin Delano Roosevelt was also influenced by socialist doctrine, although his intent might be construed as justifiable given the times. It was his responsibility to bring the nation out of a devastating depression and to that end he advanced programs such as social security and the Civilian Conservation Corps, a federally sponsored program that provided work for unemployed young men, that had more socialist leanings than democratic ones.

Executive Order 9066 was signed on February 19, 1944, which authorized the round-up of all Japanese-Americans, two-thirds of which were citizens, to imprison them in relocation camps for the duration of the war. The U.S. Supreme Court ruled this action 'unconstitutional' on December 18, 1944 but by that time tremendous trauma had been inflicted upon those whose lives had been ruined. Further confirmation of FDR's illegal actions came in 1989 when President George H.W. Bush granted financial reparation to Japanese-Americans. Roosevelt not only circumvented the Constitution, he reprehensibly broke both the legal and moral laws of the land, leading the nation yet another few yards farther from the Founding Fathers' principles.

Lyndon Baines Johnson continued the spiral of making government the Political Parent rather than leaving individual responsibility for oneself to the people of the nation when he implemented socialist-oriented plans such as Medicare and Medicaid, federally funded medical coverage for the elderly, disabled, and indigent. His rationale appeared to be for the welfare of the nation's most vulnerable citizens rather than any socialist leaning but the entitlements still served to make people dependent on government.

If we examine individual Amendments we can only conclude that America no longer values or uses the Constitution as the law of the land as it was intended and its erosion is steering the country toward a demise whose fate is that of a "one world government."

The <u>First Amendment</u> was meant to protect freedom of speech, free expression of the press, and the right to petition the government for redress of grievances.

One of the most glaring and egregious violations of the First Amendment was during the administration of Abraham Lincoln when he tyrannically and illegally suspended the Bill of Rights and the writ of habeas corpus. He blatantly displayed disdain for the Constitution as the law of the land when he jailed anyone that disagreed with him and silenced newspapers by destroying their offices and throwing their editors in jail. He also sent troops to intimidate people into not casting their vote in an effort to suppress free elections.

Since that time, other administrations have 'censored' news in various ways including not allowing the media to cover the return of bodies from the Vietnam and Gulf Wars in an effort to downplay the facts of war and manipulate government's agenda. The White House routinely suppresses facts to ensure the media 'rewrites' circumstances the way government wants them to be portrayed.

Currently, government efforts to present a biased view have been undertaken that would make it more difficult for anyone whose perspective disagrees with the views of the President and/or the Democrats in Congress. Democrats have declared war on the Republicans and the liberal Left is determined to silence the conservative Right as much as they can.

The <u>Second Amendment</u> guarantees citizens the right to keep and bear arms - <u>period</u>. It didn't put conditions or restrictions on that right. It simply guaranteed *"the right of the people to keep and bear arms"* and that that right *"shall not be infringed."* It didn't state that troops who were given guns and sent to war to fight for the freedom of America and the liberties guaranteed under the Constitution, would return only to be declared "a risk" for firearm ownership because the *government* decided war injuries had rendered them "psychologically unstable" and therefore, they should be denied gun ownership as civilians. It didn't state that certain firearms should be banned or that guns should be registered with a government that could use that registration to locate and round up those registered firearms. It didn't state that firearms could be declared "illegal" and the owner arrested if found in a vehicle within a certain range of a school. In fact, the Second Amendment was restriction free, which means actions over time to circumvent the law and render it useless, are simply unconstitutional. In their wisdom and foresight the Founders recognized that the time could come when government so flagrantly compromised the Second Amendment that firearm ownership would simply be under assault making Americans vulnerable to a dictatorship. That time has come.

Even the word 'militia' within the Second Amendment has been interpreted to mean different things over the decades and has been bastardized by current government propaganda and the liberal media to mean something evil.

George Washington stated, *"A free people…should have sufficient arms and ammunition to maintain a status of independence from any who might attempt to abuse them, which would* <u>include their own government</u>*."* From that time forward as government became more and more concerned that armed citizens might rise up against their own government, administrations have imposed ways to get around the Second Amendment in an effort to disarm the nation. There are more and more restrictions on gun sales, the ability to obtain ammunition and parts, rigid registration measures, and intimidation to disarm citizens. The new administration is circumventing the Second Amendment by coming down hard on gun related manufacturers through regulations and restrictions, which makes it impossible to obtain firearm related accessories and ammunition and thereby renders firearms useless without having to outright ban the constitutional amendment.

The biggest assault on gun ownership may be imminent with the new administration. Not only were firearms disappearing from supplier's shelves in droves as soon as Obama was elected but within the first month of his administration suppliers had virtually no ammo or accessories. Americans knew the government's assault on private citizen protection had reached a crisis point when gun related catalogs carried this disclaimer:

"Our right to "Keep and Bear Arms" is on the liberals' agenda resulting in erratic sales and astronomical price increases on ammunition, magazines, and assault weapons gear. Prices may have increased and inventories depleted from the time this catalog was printed. Please see our website for product availability and pricing. Stock up now before the inventory is forever gone."

It didn't take the new administration and the 111th Congress long to propose dictatorial legislation that would nail the coffin for rights under the Second Amendment. HR-45 would simply render the Second Amendment void. It would require a license for handguns and semiautomatic firearms, including those already in citizens' possession. Applicants must be thumb-printed and sign a certification that their gun would NOT be kept in a place where it could be used by the owner's family for self-defense. The applicant would be required to provide ALL psychiatric records, pass an exam, and pay a $25 fee. The license would have to be renewed after five years, at which time the government could revoke it. The bill would outlaw private sales and ALL gun transaction reports would be required to be filed with the Attorney General. All transactions would be subject to the Brady check, loaded firearms for self-defense would be a criminal offense, a 10-year criminal penalty and unlimited regulatory and inspection authority would be established, and vague 'crimes by omission' such as failure to report would be a 'catch-all' for anything not specifically stated in the bill. Goodbye Second Amendment; hello tyranny.

An unarmed nation is a nation heading for dictatorship. Current legislation before Congress such as HR-45 is just simply Draconian. America is no longer free and the most basic of constitutional rights is being circumvented in a round-about manner that will prevent freedom loving Americans from protecting themselves against their own government.

The Fourth Amendment provides for Warrants to protect against illegal search and seizure and the Fifth Amendment pledges due process.

Law enforcement, which was once designed to 'protect and serve' has now become a very lucrative business of profit in direct violation of the Constitution. In the early 1990s forfeiture laws were expanded to include many non-drug situations. Since then the law enforcement and legal communities have figured a way to circumvent the Fourth and Fifth Amendments of the U.S. Constitution and the necessity for warrants by simply taking **property** to *civil* court where Administrative Law places the burden of proof on the victim rather than taking a potential **suspect** to *criminal* court where Constitutional Law prevails and it is incumbent upon law enforcement to prove there actually was a crime. By going to civil court where the Constitution does not apply, cops can simply keep the booty without even charging a citizen with a crime – let alone convicting them – or providing due process to an 'alleged' suspect. In many states the Fourth and Fifth Amendments have been trampled on by law enforcement for bureaucratic greedy gain and citizens are being denied the protections promised them under the U.S. Constitution. Even worse, these actions have shamefully been allowed and sanctioned by various administrations, the Congress, and the Judicial branch of government.

The Tenth Amendment grants all powers to the states that are not clearly defined in the Constitution as being federal powers.

That all changed with Lincoln's administration. His obsession with a centralized government drove everything he did as president. He pushed his 'corporate welfare' agenda to the exclusion of what was right for the citizens of the United States and eventually placed those citizens under siege with an armed military in order to obtain his goal. States' rights got in the way of Lincoln's goal for a powerful central government so he simply went about rewriting history. Daniel Webster fabricated a theory that the federal government existed first so the states were subsequently created by the federal government and therefore, the primary power belonged to the centralized government. Lincoln embraced that ludicrous revision, thereby actually changing the intent of the Tenth Amendment. From Lincoln's tenure forward the federal government continued its thirsty quest for power, virtually swallowing up states' rights in the process, a practice that has continued to the present day.

After September 11, 2001 George W. Bush imposed extensive abuses of power through legislation, various programs, the Patriot Act and other ominous measures, which put the public at risk of innocently being persecuted contrary to everything the Founders intended. By the time Bush completed his eight-year tenure, the nation had come full circle from its fight for independence from England's tyranny. So many individual liberties had been usurped after the 9/11 attack on the nation that America was left to fight again for its independence…from invasive and unconstitutional abuses of federal power.

President Dwight D. Eisenhower observed: *"Freedom has its life in the hearts, the actions, the spirit of men and so it must be daily earned and refreshed - else like a flower cut from its life-giving roots, it will wither and die."*

The United States has abandoned the Constitution bit by bit since the administration of Andrew Jackson. Like Eisenhower's flower, the Constitution represents the "roots" of the nation and those roots have not been nourished, tended, fertilized, or watered throughout the decades. As a result, the roots have withered and died to the point they no longer support the flower and it is now wilting.

The 2008 election placed a Democratic Congress in partnership with a Democratic president, which is very likely to result in a proliferation of 'entitlement' programs and bailouts as a result of the nation's economic melt down and could enable a rapid descent back into oppression. Over 40% of America's population already lives on government dependency. In a typical election those who vote Democrat generally live off some form of government welfare while those who vote Republican generally are the taxpaying citizens. President Obama has stated over and over that he intends to develop a form of taxation that will "spread the wealth" and those that voted for him were largely those at the lower end of the economic scale who felt they would benefit from that course of action. Should Obama put that socialist policy into effect in the United States, the U.S. would surely begin a decline into the final 'oppression' and extinction stage of history's democracy cycle.

What direction does that leave for the future? The dominos are already falling if government has become so corrupted, without ethics, and lacking in a moral compass that allegiance to the Founding principles is reduced to only a 200-year old memory. To America's dismay, everything points to the fact Scottish historian Alexander Tyler may very well be right about the predictable cycles of history's governments.

The objective of this book is to take the reader on a journey through time where one can examine each presidency through the lens of the Founders and the U.S. Constitution to better understand how the nation has evolved from a Republic to a point in time that threatens the very existence of America as a free nation. It is hoped readers will be inspired to find their voice and take action to reclaim their country and restore their government to the proud manner visualized by those noble patriots from long ago.

Chapter 2

REVOLUNTIONARY WAR

The thirteen original colonies united against the British Empire in a revolution revolving around unfair taxes and cruel oppression. The armed conflict ended in 1776 with the Declaration of Independence. France was a key supporter of the colonies, providing funds, soldiers, fleets, and munitions that made a victory at Yorktown possible and ended the war.

In 1763, North Americans were subjects of the British crown so Britain imposed taxes on the American colonies to pay for the defense of America. The colonies objected because they had no representation in the British Parliament and were not even consulted. It led to the well-known phrase, "*No taxation without representation.*" Britain continued the taxes nevertheless and even added more. The Stamp Act taxed publications and the Quartering Act forced citizens to house British soldiers in American buildings. Benjamin Franklin went to Britain to plead the colonies' case against the Stamp Act and it was repealed when Britain realized a revolution would result if it continued.

The 1770 Boston Massacre in which British soldiers fired upon a mob, killing five and injuring six colony citizens, further deteriorated relations between England and the American colonies, who began boycotting British goods. It evolved into the Boston Tea Party in 1773, in which British tea was dumped into the harbor. Britain retaliated by passing the Intolerable Acts, which closed the Boston harbor until the colonies identified the culprits, which never happened.

A remarkable assembly of men now known as the Founding Fathers, feared English corruption and were steadfast in their intent to avoid it as demonstrated by the documents from the Continental Convention.

When citizen militias began forming, England sent troops to the colonies to seize firearms and arrest revolutionaries. Fighting broke out and George Washington's troops ran the British out of Boston. They fled back to England leaving the colonies in control and ready to declare independence.

The Second Continental Convention ratified the Declaration of Independence on July 2, 1776 and it was signed two days later, which became the official date of America's birth.

England created Canadian colonies for the 5% of American colonists who wanted to remain loyal to the crown and the 95% of residents left began to put their new nation in order.

Despite the overwhelming positives that resulted from the American Revolution and independence from England, two factions of the colonies actually suffered from the fledgling nation's newfound freedom. Slavery was banned in England but allowed to continue in the American colonies and the American Indians were protected under British rule but persecuted and their land stolen from them under independence from Britain.

In the end, the radical events leading up to independence and a system of laws chosen by the people, proved to be a successful "experiment in democracy" until Lincoln's term changed the basic intent of the Constitution from rule by the people to rule by centralized government.

"The Revolution was effected before the war commenced. The Revolution was in the minds and hearts of the people. This radical change in the principles, opinions, sentiments and affections of the people was the real American Revolution."

~ John Adams, 1818
2nd President of the U.S.

Chapter 3

DECLARATION OF INDEPENDENCE

The political bonds with England were officially dissolved on July 4, 1776 when the Second Continental Congress unanimously adopted the Declaration of Independence. The signers put their very lives on the line and many suffered great tragedy as a result, but they valued liberty more and were committed to preserving freedom not only for themselves, but for future generations as well.

The Declaration of Independence framed the ground rules for a moral foundation of a free society and declared citizens had the 'unalienable' right to live their lives as they wished as long as they respected the equal rights of others. This valuable document firmly instructed that government was to be run by the "Consent of the Governed" and that citizens had every right to criticize the law at any time.

Many of the same leaders who signed the Declaration of Independence also later attended the 1787 Constitutional Convention. Fifty-five delegates were present to draft and enact the document that would steer the new government – the U.S. Constitution. A delegate that stands out from the rest is George Mason, a rational, prudent gentleman of unusual vision who was born in 1725. He was an attorney and plantation owner who represented Virginia. A frequent and very influential speaker at the convention he and Patrick Henry were outspoken critics of adopting the U.S. Constitution as written because both men felt it gave the federal government too much power. Mason *declined* to sign the Constitution because he felt not enough safeguards had been put in place and the new government was destined to become a monarchy or be ruled by a corrupt oppressive aristocracy. He further complained that the House of Representatives was **not** representative of the common person and that the Senate had too much power. He was convinced the federal judiciary would destroy states' rights and that the result of the document as adopted would enable the rich to victimize, oppress, and ruin the poor. *Who says the framers had no vision for the future???*

DOCUMENT QUOTE

"...whenever any Form of Government becomes destructive of these ends, it is the Right of the People to alter or to abolish it...when a long train of abuses and usurpations [occur]...it is their right, it is their duty, to throw off such Government."

Chapter 4

BILL OF RIGHTS (1-10)

The U.S. Constitution was ratified on June 21, 1788 so the original first ten amendments to the Constitution, which are contained in the Bill of Rights, are not part of the main body of the Constitution, as they were ratified on a later date. The first ten amendments were enacted to limit the power of the federal government and were all ratified on the same date - December 15, 1791.

Amendment I	Religious freedom; freedom of speech and the press, the right to peaceful assembly, right to petition government grievances.
Amendment II	The right to keep and bear arms.
Amendment III	Housing of soldiers.
Amendment IV	The right to be secure in person, place, and things against unreasonable search and seizure. A Warrant shall be issued upon probable cause, describing the place to be searched and the person or things to be seized.
Amendment V	Rights in criminal cases. Criteria of grand jury; safeguard from double jeopardy; immunity from self incrimination; protection of due process; compensation for private property taken for public use (eminent domain).
Amendment VI	Ensures the right to a speedy jury trial in the case of criminal prosecutions as well as the right to be informed of the nature of the accusation, to confront witnesses, and obtain Counsel.

Amendment VII	Right in civil cases. Jury trial.
Amendment VIII	Prohibits excessive bail and punishment and prevents cruel and unusual punishment.
Amendment IX	Rights retained by the people.
Amendment X	Powers not assigned to the Federal government by the Constitution nor prohibited to the States by it are reserved to the States.

SUBSEQUENT AMENDMENTS (11-27)

Additional amendments were added over time and ratified individually to grant even more protection to an already insightful document.

Amendment XI	Lawsuits against States. (1795)
Amendment XII	Election of President and Vice President. (1804)
Amendment XIII	Slavery abolishment and enforcement. (1865)
Amendment XIV	Civil rights. Definition of citizenship; equal protection under the law; apportionment of representatives; prohibition of any person to hold office if they have engaged in insurrection or rebellion or have given aid or comfort to the enemy; declares illegal any debts incurred as a result of insurrection (passed as a result of the slavery issue and the Civil War). (1868)
Amendment XV	Equal voting privileges for Blacks. (1870)
Amendment XVI	Income taxes. (1913)
Amendment XVII	Direct election of U.S. Senators, and vacancies. (1913)
Amendment XVIII	Prohibition of liquor. (1919)

Amendment XIX	Womens' right to vote. (1920)
Amendment XX	Terms of President, Vice-President, Senate, and House of Representatives; Congressional sessions; emergency presidential succession. (1933)
Amendment XXI	Repeal of the Eighteenth Amendment prohibiting liquor. (1933)
Amendment XXII	Limits office of president to two terms. (1951)
Amendment XXIII	Washington, D.C. election of President and Vice-President. (1961)
Amendment XXIV	Prohibits payment of tax to qualify to vote. (1964)
Amendment XXV	Presidential succession due to removal from office, death, or resignation; filling Vice-Presidential vacancy; procedure if President is unable to discharge his duties; procedure for resumption of presidential power. (1967)
Amendment XXVI	Right to vote at eighteen. (1971)
Amendment XXVII	Congressional salaries. (1992)

Chapter 5

1787 CONSTITUTIONAL CONVENTION

Drafting the guidelines for a new government was an awesome responsibility and involved many heated debates as the Founders were well aware of the strengths and weaknesses of a democratic union as opposed to a Republic. There were voices for and against the Federalist Papers with the Federalists wanting a more pure democracy that leaned toward protecting the rights of elitists, while Anti-Federalists favored a Republic that represented all strata of the common citizen. The 55 delegates' amazing insight into human nature demonstrates how little things have changed in two centuries in both political ethics and social attitude – and how well Anti-Federalist delegates understood the possibility of today's appalling social, political, and economic climate. To read both views of the actual debates of the delegates framing the roadmap of the new government, go to http://odur.et.rug.nl/~usa/D/1776-1800/federalist/fedxx.htm.

Alexander Hamilton was one of the main authors of the Federalist Papers, which were published to influence the public toward adopting *his* view of the Constitution. Hamilton was an elitist who disdained the common person and believed in a superior centralized authority where the President would appoint state governors. Senators and the President would hold office for life and Congress would have exclusive authority to make ALL laws. His vision was self-serving and he favored England's style of government so it was clear he leaned toward the very monarchy the Anti-Federalists warned against.

A Republic entails government of the people who elect representatives that are granted *limited* authority to enact only what the voters deem them to do. It is designed to protect the rights of the common person. The Constitution was primarily based on this view but obviously, over time it has been drastically circumvented.

Patrick Henry was an Anti-Federalist that fought hard for equal and fair representation for the every day citizen. He had a clear vision of what could happen in the future if a Republic form of government was not adopted. He was passionate and emphatic in his pleas in trying to make his fellow framers understand the pitfalls of what they eventually ratified.

In 1954, Senator William Jenner woefully observed that, "*...outwardly we have a Constitutional government but we have operating within our government and political system, another body representing another form of government, a bureaucratic elite which believes our Constitution is outmoded. This group is going to make us over to suit their pleasure...it has its own local political support organizations, its own pressure groups, its own vested interests, its foothold within our government, and its own propaganda apparatus.*" Pretty scary food for thought but it is obviously happening right now – today.

Chapter 6

INTRODUCTION TO THE CONSTITUTION OF THE UNITED STATES

The Declaration of Independence was created on September 17, 1787 and ratified on June 21, 1788. It sets forth the *principles* of the nation.

The U.S. Constitution followed as the fundamental supreme *law* of the land when it was ratified on June 21, 1788. Its terms transcend time and were meant to guide generations to come – if only we would follow them. The primary goal was to establish a government where all power came from the people and representatives of the people had limited power. It clearly states that any representative of the people is to act only on their behalf.

Article I outlines the authority of the U.S. House of Representatives and the U.S. Senate. Article II delves into the power of the executive branch and Article III presents the perimeters of the judicial system. This system of checks and balances was one of the most crucial components of the document in an effort to prevent an oppressive government. The concept of separating the three main branches of government as a means of checks and balances contains a flaw, however. The President is elected to the executive branch. Representatives are elected to the legislative branch. But the judicial branch is not elected. The president appoints the U.S. Supreme Court judges and that flaw has and does create a conflict of interest that is detrimental to the intent of the separation of power. Selections for the judicial branch of government should be achieved through a process separate from the executive branch. As time progressed, the intent of the Founding Fathers has been circumvented and the birth certificate of our nation is now under attack and in grave danger.

In an effort to limit the power of the federal government, the Bill of Rights was ratified on December 15, 1791 and the first ten amendments convey that purpose. With time and historical events, however, power became more and more centralized as states rights dwindled.

The Founders drafted an extraordinary document that could serve us well even today – BUT – if America is to remain a free society it is up to leaders to honor their oath of office and for the people of the nation to be vigilant against those who don't. The burning passion for freedom must remain alive and active in the hearts and minds of citizens if they are to keep freedom alive for themselves and the generations to follow.

Chapter 7

THE CONSTITUTION OF THE UNITED STATES

We the People* of the United States, in Order to form a more perfect Union, establish Justice, insure domestic Tranquility, provide for the common defence, (sp) promote the general Welfare, and secure the Blessings of Liberty to ourselves and our Posterity, do ordain and establish this Constitution for the United States of America.

> *The original document had no title and simply began "We the People."
>
> The spelling of certain words used at the time has not been changed.

ARTICLE I

Section 1. All legislative Powers herein granted shall be vested in a Congress of the United States, which shall consist of a Senate and House of Representatives.

Section 2.   The House of Representatives shall be composed of Members chosen every second Year by the People of the several States, and the Electors in each State shall have the Qualifications requisite for Electors of the most numerous Branch of the State Legislature.

No Person shall be a Representative who shall not have attained to the Age of twenty-five Years, and been seven Years a Citizen of the United States, and who shall not, when elected, be an Inhabitant of that State in which he shall be chosen.

Representatives and direct Taxes shall be apportioned among the several States which may be included within this Union, according to their respective Numbers, which shall be determined by adding to the whole Number of free Persons, including those bound to Service for a Term of Years, and excluding Indians not taxed, three-fifths of all other Persons. The actual Enumeration shall be made within three Years after the first Meeting of the Congress of the United States, and within every subsequent Term of ten Years, in such Manner as they shall by Law direct. The Number of Representatives shall not exceed one for every thirty Thousand, but each State shall have at Least one Representative; and until such enumeration shall be made, the State of New Hampshire shall be entitled to chuse (sp) three, Massachusetts eight, Rhode-Island and Providence Plantations one, Connecticut five, New York six, New Jersey four, Pennsylvania eight, Delaware one, Maryland six, Virginia ten, North Carolina five, South Carolina five, and Georgia three.

When vacancies happen in the Representation from any State, the Executive Authority thereof shall issue Writs of Election to fill such Vacancies.

The House of Representatives shall chuse (sp) their Speaker and other Officers; and shall have the sole Power of Impeachment.

Section 3. The Senate of the United States shall be composed of two Senators from each State, chosen by the Legislature thereof, for six Years; and each Senator shall have one Vote.

Immediately after they shall be assembled in Consequence of the first Election, they shall be divided as equally as may be into three Classes. The Seats of the Senators of the first Class shall be vacated at the Expiration of the second Year, of the second Class at the Expiration of the fourth Year, and of the third Class at the Expiration of the sixth Year, so that one third may be chosen every second Year; and if Vacancies happen by Resignation, or otherwise, during the Recess of the Legislature of any State, the Executive thereof may make temporary Appointments until the next Meeting of the Legislature, which shall then fill such Vacancies.

No Person shall be a Senator who shall not have attained to the Age of thirty Years, and been nine Years a Citizen of the United States, and who shall not, when elected, be an Inhabitant of that State for which he shall be chosen.

The Vice President of the United States shall be President of the Senate, but shall have no Vote, unless they be equally divided.

The Senate shall chuse (sp) their other Officers, and also a President pro tempore, in the Absence of the Vice President, or when he shall exercise the Office of President of the United States.

The Senate shall have the sole Power to try all Impeachments. When sitting for that Purpose, they shall be on Oath or Affirmation. When the President of the United States is tried, the Chief Justice shall preside; And no Person shall be convicted without the Concurrence of two thirds of the Members present.

Judgment in Cases of Impeachment shall not extend further than to removal from Office, and disqualification to hold and enjoy any Office of honor, Trust or Profit under the United States: but the Party convicted shall nevertheless be liable and subject to Indictment, Trial, Judgment and Punishment, according to Law.

Section 4. The Times, Places and Manner of holding Elections for Senators and Representatives, shall be prescribed in each State by the Legislature thereof; but the Congress may at any time by Law make or alter such Regulations, except as to the Places of chusing (sp) Senators.

The Congress shall assemble at least once in every Year, and such Meeting shall be on the first Monday in December, unless they shall by Law appoint a different Day.

Section 5. Each House shall be the Judge of Elections, Returns and Qualifications of its own Members, and a Majority of each shall constitute a Quorum to do Business; but a smaller Number may adjourn from day to day, and may be authorized to compel the Attendance of absent Members, in such Manner, and under such Penalties as each House may provide.

Each House may determine the Rules of its Proceedings, punish its Members for disorderly Behaviour, (sp) and, with the Concurrence of two thirds, expel a Member.

Each House shall keep a Journal of its Proceedings, and from time to time publish the same, excepting such Parts as may in their Judgment require Secrecy; and the Yeas and Nays of the Members of either House on any question shall, at the Desire of one fifth of those Present, be entered on the Journal.

Neither House, during the Session of Congress, shall, without the Consent of the other, adjourn for more than three days, nor to any other Place than that in which the two Houses shall be sitting.

Section 6. The Senators and Representatives shall receive a Compensation for their Services, to be ascertained by Law, and paid out of the Treasury of the United States. They shall in all Cases, except Treason, Felony and Breach of the Peace, be privileged from Arrest during their Attendance at the Session of their respective House, and in going to and returning from the same; and for any Speech or Debate in either House they shall not be questioned in any other Place.

No Senator or Representative shall, during the Time for which he was elected, be appointed to any civil Office under the Authority of the United States which shall have been created, or the Emoluments whereof shall have been encreased (sp) during such time; and no Person holding any Office under the United States, shall be a Member of either House during his Continuance of Office.

Section 7. All Bills for raising Revenue shall originate in the House of Representatives; but the Senate may propose or concur with Amendments as on other Bills.

Every Bill which shall have passed the House of Representatives and the Senate, shall, before it comes a Law, be presented to the President of the United States; if he approve he shall sign it, but if not he shall return it, with his Objections to that House in which it shall have originated, who shall enter the Objections at large on their Journal, and proceed to reconsider it. If after such Reconsideration two thirds of that House shall agree to pass the Bill, it shall be sent, together with the Objections, to the other House, by which it shall likewise be reconsidered, and if approved by two thirds of that House, it shall become a Law. But in all such Cases the Votes of both Houses shall be determined by Yeas and Nays, and the Names of Persons voting for and against the Bill shall be entered on the Journal of each House respectively. If any Bill shall not be returned by the President within ten Days (Sundays excepted) after it shall have been presented to him, the Same shall be a Law, in like Manner as if he signed it, unless the Congress by their Adjournment prevent its Return, in which Case it shall not be a Law.

Every Order, Resolution, or Vote to which the Concurrence of the Senate and House of Representatives may be necessary (except on a question of Adjournment) shall be presented to the President of the United States; and before the Same shall take Effect, shall be approved by him; or being disapproved by him, shall be repassed by two thirds of the Senate and House of Representatives, according to the Rules and Limitations prescribed in the Case of a Bill.

Section 8. The Congress shall have Power To lay and collect Taxes, Duties, Imposts and Excises, to pay the Debts and provide for the common Defence (sp) and general Welfare of the United States; but all Duties, Imposts and Excises shall be uniform throughout the United States.

To borrow Money on the credit of the United States;

To regulate Commerce with foreign Nations, and among the several States, and with the Indian Tribes;

To establish an uniform Rule of Naturalization, and uniform Laws on the subject of Bankruptcies throughout the United States;

To coin Money, regulate the Value thereof, and of foreign Coin, and fix the Standard of Weights and Measures;

To provide for the Punishment of counterfeiting the Securities and current Coin of the United States;

To establish Post Offices and post Roads;

To promote the Progress of Science and useful Arts, by securing for limited Times to Authors, and Inventors the exclusive Right to their respective Writings and Discoveries;

To constitute Tribunals inferior to the supreme Court;

To define and punish Piracies and Felonies committed on the high Seas, and Offences against the Law of Nations;

To declare War, grant Letters of Marque and Reprisal, and make Rules concerning Captures on Land and Water;

To raise and support Armies, but no Appropriation of Money to that Use shall be for a longer Term than two years;

To provide and maintain a Navy;

To make Rules for the Government and Regulation of the land and naval Forces;

To provide for calling forth the Militia to execute the Laws of the Union, suppress Insurrections and repel Invasions;

To provide for organizing, arming, and disciplining, the Militia, and for governing such Part of them as may be employed in the Service of the United States, reserving to the States respectively, the Appointment of the Officers, and the Authority of training the Militia according to the discipline prescribed by Congress;

To exercise exclusive Legislation in all Cases whatsoever, over such District (not exceeding ten Miles square) as may, by Cession of particular States, and the Acceptance of Congress, become the Seat of the Government of the United States, and to exercise like Authority over all Places purchased by the Consent of the Legislature of the State in which the Same shall be, for the Erection of Forts, Magazines, Arsenals, dock-Yards, and other needful Buildings; - And

To make all Laws which shall be necessary and proper for carrying into Execution the foregoing Powers, and all other Powers vested by this Constitution in the Government of the United States, or in any Department or Office thereof.

Section 9. The Migration or Importation of such Persons as any of the States now existing shall think proper to admit, shall not be prohibited by the Congress prior to the Year one thousand eight hundred and eight, but a Tax or duty may be imposed on such Importation, not exceeding ten dollars for each Person.

The Privilege of the Writ of Habeas Corpus shall not be suspended, unless when in Cases of Rebellion or Invasion the public Safety may require it.

No Bill of Attainder or ex post facto Law shall be passed.

No Capitation, or other direct, Tax shall be laid, unless in Proportion to the Census or Enumeration hereinbefore directed to be taken.

No Tax or Duty shall be laid on Articles exported from any State. No Preference shall be given by any Regulation of Commerce or Revenue to the Ports of one State over those of another; nor shall Vessels bound to, or from, one State, be obliged to enter, clear, or pay Duties in another.

No Money shall be drawn from the Treasury, but in Consequence of Appropriations made by Law; and a regular Statement and Account of the Receipts and Expenditures of all public Money shall be published from time to time.

No Title of Nobility shall be granted by the United States; and no Person holding any Office of Profit or Trust under them, shall, without the Consent of the Congress, accept of any present, Emolument, Office, or Title, of any kind whatever, from any King, Prince, or foreign State.

Section 10. No State shall enter into any Treaty, Alliance, or Confederation; grant Letters of Marque or Reprisal; coin Money; emit Bills of Credit; make any Thing but gold and silver Coin a Tender in Payment of Debts; pass any Bill of Attainder, ex post facto Law, or Law impairing the Obligation of Contracts, or grant any Title of Nobility.

No State shall, without the Consent of the Congress, lay any Imposts or Duties on Imports or Exports, except what may be absolutely necessary for executing its inspections Laws; and the net Produce of all Duties and Imposts, laid by any State on Imports or Exports, shall be for the Use of the Treasury of the United States; and all such Laws shall be subject to the Revision and Control of the Congress.

No State shall, without the Consent of Congress, lay any Duty on Tonnage, keep Troops, or Ships of War in time of Peace, enter into any Agreement or Compact with another State, or with a foreign Power, or engage in War, unless actually invaded, or in such imminent Danger as will not admit of delay.

ARTICLE II

Section 1. The executive Power shall be vested in a President of the United States of America. He shall hold his Office during the Term of four Years, and, together with the Vice President, chosen for the same Term, be elected as follows:

Each State shall appoint, in such Manner as the Legislature thereof may direct, a Number of Electors, equal to the whole Number of Senators and Representatives to which the State may be entitled in the Congress: but no Senator or Representative, or Person holding an Office of Trust or Profit under the United States, shall be appointed an Elector.

The Electors shall meet in their respective States, and vote by Ballot for two Persons, of whom one at least shall not be an Inhabitant of the same State with themselves. And they shall make a List of all the Persons voted for, and of the Number of Votes for each; which List they shall sign and certify, and transmit sealed to the Seat of the Government of the United States, directed to the President of the Senate. The President of the Senate shall, in the Presence of the Senate and House of Representatives, open all the Certificates, and the Votes shall then be counted. The Person having the greatest Number of Votes shall be the President, if such Number be a Majority of the whole Number of Electors appointed; and if there be more than one who have such Majority, and have an equal Number of Votes, then the House of Representatives shall immediately chuse (sp) by Ballot one of them for President; and if no Person have a Majority, then from the five highest on the List the said House shall in like Manner chuse (sp) the President. But in chusing (sp) the President, the Votes shall be taken by States, the Representatives from each State having one Vote; A quorum for this Purpose shall consist of a Member or Members from two thirds of the States, and a Majority of all the States shall be necessary to a Choice. In every Case, after the Choice of the President, the Person having the greatest Number of Votes of the Electors shall be the Vice President. But if there shall remain two or more who have equal Votes, the Senate shall chuse (sp) from them by Ballot the Vice President.

The Congress may determine the Time of Choosing the Electors, and the Day on which they shall give their Votes: which Day shall be the same throughout the United States.

No Person except a natural born Citizen, or a Citizen of the United States, at the time of the Adoption of this Constitution, shall be eligible to the Office of President; neither shall any Person be eligible to that Office who shall not have attained to the Age of Thirty five Years, and been fourteen Years a Resident within the United States.

In Case of the Removal of the President from Office, or of his Death, Resignation, or Inability to discharge the Powers and Duties of the said Office, the Same shall devolve on the Vice President, and the Congress may by Law provide for the Case of Removal, Death, Resignation or Inability, both of the President and Vice President, declaring what Officer shall then act as President, and such Officer shall act accordingly, until the Disability be removed, or a President shall be elected.

The President shall, at stated Times, receive for his Services, a Compensation, which shall neither be encreased (sp) nor diminished during the Period for which he shall have been elected, and he shall not receive within that Period any other Emolument from the United States, or any of them.

Before he enter on the Execution of his Office, he shall take the following Oath or Affirmation: -- "I do solemnly swear (or affirm) that I will faithfully execute the Office of President of the United States, and will to the best of my Ability, preserve, protect and defend the Constitution of the United States."

Section 2. The President shall be Commander in Chief of the Army and Navy of the United States, and of the Militia of the several States, when called into the actual Service of the United States; he may require the Opinion, in writing, of the principal Officer in each of the executive Departments, upon any Subject relating to the Duties of their respective Offices, and he shall have Power to grant Reprieves and Pardons for Offenses against the United States, except in Cases of Impeachment.

He shall have Power, by and with the Advice and Consent of the Senate, to make Treaties, provided two thirds of the Senators present concur; and he shall nominate, and by and with the Advice and Consent of the Senate, shall appoint Ambassadors, other public Ministers and Consuls, Judges of the supreme Court, and all other Officers of the United States, whose Appointments are not herein otherwise provided for, and which shall be established by Law; but the Congress may by Law vest the Appointment of such inferior Officers, as they think proper, in the President alone, in the Courts of Law, or in the Heads of Departments.

The President shall have Power to fill up all Vacancies that may happen during the Recess of the Senate, by granting Commissions which shall expire at the End of their next Session.

Section 3. He shall from time to time give to the Congress Information of the State of the Union, and recommend to their Consideration such Measures as he shall judge necessary and expedient; he may, on extraordinary Occasions, convene both Houses, or either of them, and in Case of Disagreement between them, with Respect to the Time of Adjournment, he may adjourn them to such Time as he shall think proper; he shall receive Ambassadors and other public Ministers; he shall take Care that the Laws be faithfully executed, and shall Commission all the Officers of the United States.

Section 4. The President, Vice President and all civil Officers of the United States, shall be removed from Office on impeachment for, and Conviction of, Treason, Bribery, or other high Crimes and Misdemeanors.

ARTICLE III

Section 1. The judicial Power of the United States, shall be vested in one supreme Court, and in such inferior Courts as the Congress may from time to time ordain and establish. The Judges, both of the supreme and inferior Courts, shall hold their Offices during good Behaviour, (sp) and shall, at stated Times, receive for their Services, a Compensation, which shall not be diminished during their Continuance in Office.

Section 2. The judicial Power shall extend to all Cases, in Law and Equity, arising under this Constitution, the Laws of the United States, and Treaties made, or which shall be made, under their Authority; -- to all Cases affecting Ambassadors, other public Ministers and Consuls; -- to all Cases of admiralty and maritime Jurisdiction – to Controversies to which the United States shall be a Party; -- to Controversies between two or more States; -- between a State and Citizens of another State; -- between Citizens of different States; -- between Citizens of the same State claiming Lands under Grants of different States, and between a State, or the Citizens thereof, and foreign States, Citizens or Subjects.

In all Cases affecting Ambassadors, other public Ministers and Consuls, and those in which a State shall be Party, the supreme Court shall have original Jurisdiction. In all the other Cases before mentioned, the supreme Court shall have appellate Jurisdiction, both as to Law and Fact, with such Exceptions, and under such Regulations as the Congress shall make.

The Trial of all Crimes, except in Cases of Impeachment, shall be by Jury; and such Trial shall be held in the State where the said Crime shall have been committed; but when not committed within any State, the Trial shall be at such Place or Places as the Congress may by Law have directed.

Section 3. Treason against the United States, shall consist only in levying War against them, or in adhering to their Enemies, giving them Aid and Comfort. No Person shall be convicted of Treason unless on the Testimony of two Witnesses to the same overt Act, or on Confession in open Court.

The Congress shall have Power to declare the Punishment of Treason, but no Attainder of Treason shall work Corruption of Blood, or Forfeiture except during the Life of the Person attained.

ARTICLE IV

Section 1. Full Faith and Credit shall be given in each State to the public Acts, Records, and judicial Proceedings of every other State. And the Congress may by general Laws prescribe the Manner in which such Acts, Records and Proceedings shall be proved, and the Effect thereof.

Section 2. The Citizens of each State shall be entitled to all Privileges and Immunities of Citizens in the several States.

A Person charged in any State with Treason, Felony, or other Crime, who shall flee from Justice, and be found in another State, shall on Demand of the executive Authority of the State from which he fled, be delivered up, to be removed to the State having Jurisdiction of the Crime.

No Person held to Service or Labour (sp) in one State, under the Laws thereof, escaping into another, shall, in Consequence of any Law or Regulation therein, be discharged from such Service or Labour, (sp) but shall be delivered up on Claim of the Party to whom such Service or Labour (sp) may be due.

Section 3. New States may be admitted by the Congress into this Union; but no new State shall be formed or erected within the Jurisdiction of any other State; nor any State be formed by the Junction of two or more States, or Parts of States, without the Consent of the Legislatures of the States concerned as well as of the Congress.

The Congress shall have Power to dispose of and make all needed Rules and Regulations respecting the Territory or other Property belonging to the United States; and nothing in this Constitution shall be construed as to Prejudice any Claims of the United States, or of any particular State.

Section 4. The United States shall guarantee to every State in this Union a Republican Form of Government, and shall protect each of them against Invasion; and on Application of the Legislature, or of the Executive (when the Legislature cannot be convened) against domestic Violence.

ARTICLE V

The Congress whenever two thirds of both Houses shall deem it necessary, shall propose Amendments to this Constitution, or, on the Application of the Legislatures of two thirds of the several States, shall call a Convention for proposing Amendments, which, in either Case, shall be valid to all Intents and Purposes, as Part of this Constitution, when ratified by the Legislatures of three fourths of the several States, or by Conventions in three fourths thereof, as the one or the other Mode of Ratification may be proposed by the Congress; Provided that no Amendment which may be made prior to the Year One thousand eight hundred and eight shall in any Manner affect the first and fourth Clauses in the Ninth Section of the first Article; and that no State, without its Consent, shall be deprived of its equal Suffrage in the Senate.

ARTICLE VI

All Debts contracted and Engagements entered into, before the Adoption of this Constitution, shall be as valid against the United States under this Constitution, as under the Confederation.

This Constitution and the Laws of the United States which shall be made in Pursuance thereof; and all Treaties made, or which shall be made, under the Authority of the United States, shall be the supreme Law of the Land; and the Judges in every State shall be bound thereby, and Thing in the Constitution or Laws of any State to the Contrary notwithstanding.

The Senators and Representatives before mentioned, and the Members of the several State Legislatures, and all executive and judicial Officers, both of the United States and of the several States, shall be bound by Oath or Affirmation, to support this Constitution; but no religious Test shall ever be required as a Qualification to any Office or public Trust under the United States.

ARTICLE VII

The Ratification of the Conventions of nine States, shall be sufficient for the Establishment of this Constitution between the States so ratifying the Same.

Done in Convention by the Unanimous Consent of the States present the Seventeenth Day of September in the Year of our Lord one thousand seven hundred and Eighty seven and of the Independence of the United States of America the Twelfth IN WITNESS whereof We have hereunto subscribed our Names,

GEORGE WASHINGTON, President
And Deputy from Virginia,

In CONVENTION,
Monday, September 17th, 1787

PRESENT

The States of New-Hampshire, Massachusetts, Connecticut, Mr. Hamilton from New-York, New-Jersey, Pennsylvania, Delaware, Maryland, Virginia, North-Carolina, South-Carolina and Georgia:

RESOLVED,

That the preceding Constitution be laid before the United States in Congress assembled, and that it is the opinion of this Convention, that it should afterwards be submitted to a Convention of Delegates, chosen in each State by the People thereof, under the Recommendation of its Legislature, for their Assent and Ratification; and that each Convention assenting to, and ratifying the Same, should give Notice thereof to the United States in Congress assembled.

Resolved, That it is the Opinion of this Convention, that as soon as the Conventions of nine States shall have ratified this Constitution, the United States in Congress assembled should fix a Day on which Electors should be appointed by the States which shall have ratified the same, and a Day on which the Electors should assemble to vote for the President, and the Time and Place for commencing Proceedings under this Constitution. That after such Publication the Electors should be appointed, and the Senators and Representatives elected: That the Electors should meet on the Day fixed for the Election of the President, and should transmit their Votes certified, signed, sealed and directed, as the Constitution requires, to the Secretary of the United States in Congress assembled, that the Senators and Representatives should convene at the Time and Place assigned; that the Senators should appoint a President of the Senate, for the sole Purpose of receiving, opening and counting the Votes for President; and, that after he shall be chosen, the Congress, together with the President, should, without Delay, proceed to execute this Constitution.

By the Unanimous Order of the Convention,

GEORGE WASHINGTON, President.
William Jackson, Secretary

Chapter 8

PRESIDENTIAL OVERVIEWS

The presidential oath is short but all encompassing. From Article II, Section I of the U.S. Constitution, forty-four men deemed exceptional enough by American citizens to be entrusted to represent and protect them while serving in the highest office in the land have proclaimed:

"I do solemnly swear (or affirm) that I will faithfully execute the office of President of the United States, and will to the best of my ability, preserve, protect and defend the Constitution of the United States."

While many books extol the virtues of those who have occupied the Oval Office, few include the less than heroic side of some presidents for fear of 'offending' the office of the presidency. A wise person once said that not only should the office of president be respected, but the person occupying that office should *earn* respect as well. President Theodore Roosevelt went even further when he stated, *"To announce that there must be no criticism of the President is morally treasonable to the American public."* The following synopsis of each president is meant to be objective but will delve into the negative side of presidential personalities and behavior if it helps the reader better understand how each administration did or did not honor the guidelines of the U.S. Constitution as promised in their Oath of Office. Every effort toward an unbiased view has been made in examining why specific things took place during a particular administration and how that occurrence affected a president's ability as Chief Executive and impacted on the American public and its history. It is hoped the reader will keep an open mind when the light of truth is focused on mere human beings who had the misfortune of being viewed as larger than life and put on impossible pedestals.

Examining each president is like looking at the nation's family album. It portrays an image of diversified people who were instrumental in establishing history and making America what it is today. Each president contributed his own distinctive influence on the nation's rich heritage but this book seeks to also show each president as a mortal man, subject to greatness as well as human setbacks. The following overviews will analyze each man for his own unique imprint on history as well as his very human warts and imperfections.

GEORGE WASHINGTON

1732 - 1799

First President of the United States

Presidential term: 1789-1797. Washington was a Federalist who favored a strong central government but held no official party affiliation as America's first president. Aloof by nature, he was a soldier and plantation owner who was more concerned with status and benefits for the wealthy than improving life for the 'common' class. As the nation's first president, he faced an overwhelming and humbling task in forging the Office of the President.

The cornerstone for the White House was laid in October 1792 and the residence consisted of a gray sandstone box measuring 165 feet east to west and 85 feet north to south and was simply referred to as the "President's House." The first president never lived in the mansion, however, as it was not completed until the second president's term of office.

Washington presided over the Constitutional Convention in Philadelphia that drafted the U.S. Constitution in 1787 and was the only president to receive 100% of the electoral votes. Washington chose not to associate himself with any political party because he felt a two party system would only result in conflict within the governmental and political processes. A reluctant president, he also set the precedent of only two-terms for the executive office with the standard later becoming law by way of passage of the 22nd Amendment to the Constitution.

Washington trod on virgin ground when he took office as no one actually understood what the new nation and its government would look like. His first term of office was spent simply organizing the new government and establishing a blueprint from which the new government would function.

Martha Washington made the president's job a bit more difficult when she tried to instill an imperial tone to the presidency by insisting those in her presence curtsey to her but Washington shunned regal titles opting for the simple description of 'President.'

His second term was turbulent due to the treaty with Britain that was negotiated by John Jay. While it successfully addressed business issues, it failed to prevent Britain from stopping American ships at sea and kidnapping American seamen, which created hostile criticism for Washington.

In 1794, the president sent federal troops to Pennsylvania to quell a rebellion over federal taxes on homemade whiskey. By that time, he wanted nothing to do with a third term and retired to his property at Mount Vernon.

Washington was held in high regard and is the only president to have a state and a nation's capital named after him.

JOHN ADAMS

1735 –1826

Second President of the United States

Presidential term: 1797-1801. Federalist Party. Adams was a lawyer and the first president to live in the president's mansion. In 1797 the building received a coat of whitewash and the public began informally referring to it as the "White House." His wife, Abigail, was one of the most intellectual and spirited First Ladies and considered ahead of her time when it came to women's issues.

As did the first president, Adams believed in a centralized government and had an on-going dispute with his vice president, Thomas Jefferson, who believed in a state's rights concept. Nevertheless, both men worked well together as brilliant contributors to the creation of the nation's blueprint, the Declaration of Independence.

The dislike between Adams and Jefferson over their different views regarding where the seat of power should be, resulted in petty retribution by Adams when he lost reelection to Jefferson. To Jefferson's dismay, Adams staffed federal offices and judicial positions with Federalists just before leaving office and then left Washington at dawn to avoid Jefferson's inauguration. Ironically, the two lifelong adversaries became close friends in their old age through correspondence and died on the same day...the 50th anniversary of the signing of the Declaration of Independence. They were the only two signers to also become president.

Prior to his presidency, Adams spent ten years in diplomatic service to France where he was exposed to European royal courts. That caused him to adopt monarchial tendencies and view government as an institution that should be run by only the rich and elite. He considered himself superior to most people and that pompous opinion and his temperamental personality constantly put him at odds with those whose good will he needed to accomplish important issues as president. Nevertheless, genuine love for his country and the new system of government led him to be one of the wisest and most protective of a free way of life of any of the American presidents.

Due to his respect for freedom, it is confusing that Adams would strike a blow to democracy by passing the Alien and Sedition Act in 1798, which banned criticism of the government and jeopardized freedoms guaranteed under the Bill of Rights. The President abused his authority by using the Act to jail newspaper editors, including Benjamin Franklin's grandson who was a newspaperman, simply for things they wrote about America. After becoming president, Thomas Jefferson declared three of the four Acts unconstitutional and voided them.

Adams is seen by history to be an important figure in helping to create the United States' form of government but viewed largely as an ineffective president due to his difficult personality.

THOMAS JEFFERSON

1743 - 1826

Third President of the United States

Presidential term: 1801-1809. Democratic-Republican Party. Jefferson was an attorney, plantation owner, and diplomat.

He was a strong advocate of states' rights, limited federal government, separation of church and state, defender of human liberty, and consent of the governed. His view of ideal government was "...*one that not only prohibits individuals in society from infringing on the liberty of other individuals, but also restrains **itself** from diminishing individual liberty.*"

Named the "Man of the People," he was best known as the author of the Declaration of Independence.

He objected to the final version of the U.S. Constitution in which those involved in writing it gave too much concentration of power to the government rather than the people but he agreed to the wording when he learned the Bill of Rights would be added.

As Washington's Secretary of State, Jefferson was constantly at odds with Treasury Secretary Alexander Hamilton who was an aristocrat that believed in centralized government while Jefferson saw the nation as comprised of every day people and supported state's rights. Their feud led to the two-party system, something the founders didn't envision when they framed the Constitution. Jefferson was the founder of the Democratic-Republican Party, which was the predecessor of the modern day Democratic Party.

The Louisiana Purchase, Lewis and Clark Expedition, and the first Barbary Coast War were major events during his administration. The opening line of the Marine's Hymn includes the words, "...*the shores of Tripoli*," which refers to the first Barbary Coast War. Barbary pirates and slave traders were obstructing trade between the U.S. and the Tripoli region, as well as taking American prisoners. Jefferson sent the U.S. Marines and Navy to invade Tripoli in 1805 to free American prisoners and end piracy in that region. A staunch gun advocate, Jefferson said, *"Laws that forbid the carrying of arms...disarm only those who are neither inclined nor determined to commit crimes...for an unarmed man may be attacked with greater confidence than an armed man."*

While living in the White House, the first iron cook stove made life easier for Jefferson's staff in 1801 when it replaced an open fireplace. Jefferson undoubtedly enjoyed the installation of two custom made "water closets" in 1803 that replaced the unpleasant outdoor privy.

Although John Adams and Thomas Jefferson had a long standing disagreement regarding the basic seat of power of government, they became close friends later in life and ironically, died within hours of each other on the 4th of July - the 50th anniversary of the signing of the Declaration of Independence.

JAMES MADISON

1751 - 1836

Fourth President of the United States

Presidential term: 1809-1817. Democratic-Republican Party. Madison was a lawyer and a Founding Father of our nation. While working in Virginia against President Adams' Alien and Sedition Acts, he wrote a resolution that said states had the right to reject federal law and also helped draft the state constitution of Virginia which became the model for the U.S. Constitution. His administration was distinguished from others in that both his vice presidents died while in office.

He felt the final wording of the Constitution gave too much power to the central government and too much privilege to the wealthy. Known as the "Father of the Constitution," he was the author of the first ten amendments to the Constitution and principal author of the Constitution of the United States itself. The Bill of Rights was not part of the main body of the Constitution and did not apply to the states until passage of the 14th and 15th Amendments, which restricted the power of the states. As a framer and defender of the Constitution, Madison fought against aristocracy, wanted limited federal power, separation of power in the form of strong checks and balances among the three branches of government, and limited special interest influence.

America declared war on Britain in 1812 for seizing thousands of American sailors to inflate the British navy. Additionally, Britain placed restrictions on neutral trade during the time they were at war with France, supported American Indians in their defense of tribal land against intruding settlers which angered Americans, and the British desired to expand American territories. Americans were determined to drive the British out of North America but the war effort was very disorganized and dragged on for over two-and-a-half years, during which time Washington, D.C. and the President's

Mansion were burned. The president's wife, Dolley, was revered for saving Stuart's portrait of President Washington when the British burned the White House.

The British then set out to capture Baltimore but were unable to destroy Fort McHenry, which was located at the entrance to the harbor. After 25 hours of bombarding the fort, the British left. Defense of the fort inspired Francis Scott Key to write "The Star Spangled Banner."

The war solved nothing. No territory was lost or gained by either the Americans or the British and none of the contested disputes were addressed. The issue of American sailors being seized by the British navy ceased to exist with the British defeat of Napoleon. In fact, after the war, the United States and Britain remained relatively peaceful and America was treated as an independent power by Britain and Madison enjoyed renewed popularity for the remainder of his term.

Dolley Madison was the earliest First Lady to be involved as an advisor in presidential matters and was known as an exceptional hostess. Life became much easier for the residence when two wells were installed in 1814 eliminating the need to fetch water a half-mile from the White House.

JAMES MONROE

1758 - 1831

Fifth President of the United States

Presidential term: 1817-1825. Democratic-Republican Party. Monroe was a plantation owner.

An Anti-federalist, he opposed Senate power and authorizing direct taxes in the Constitution.

President Jefferson sent Monroe to France where he successfully negotiated the Louisiana Purchase from Napoleon. That led to a later appointment by President Madison as Secretary of State and then Secretary of War in 1814, which brought peace and prosperity and catapulted Monroe to the presidency.

The "Panic of 1819" was considered the first major financial depression in U.S. history and was a stressful time in his presidency. Nevertheless, Monroe infused some light-hearted cheerfulness with the marriage of his daughter who was the first person to be married in the White House.

Monroe was strong in foreign affairs and was responsible for the Monroe Doctrine, which opposed European interference in American matters.

After leaving office, Monroe was the third president to die on the fourth of July, although in a different year than John Adams and Thomas Jefferson.

JOHN QUINCY ADAMS

1767 - 1848

Sixth President of the United States

Presidential term: 1825-1829. Federalist, Democratic-Republican Party, National Republican Party, and later, the Anti-Masonic, and Whig Parties. Adams was the son of second president John Adams. A lawyer and diplomat, his administration was marked by bitter in-fighting that kept the president from accomplishing much of note.

Adams ran against four formidable opponents for the 1828 election. Henry Clay was Speaker of the House, William Crawford was Secretary of the Treasury, Andrew Jackson was a U.S. Senator, and John Calhoun was Secretary of War. Crawford suffered an debilitating stroke and none of the remaining candidates won a majority of the popular or electoral votes so the decision of who would be president rested with the U.S. House of Representatives under the terms of the 12th Amendment. Clay did not place in the top three choices so he was declared ineligible whereupon he threw his support behind Adams who became the choice for president. Adams appointed Clay Secretary of State, which outraged Andrew Jackson and his supporters. They accused Adams and Clay of forging a "corrupt deal" and that allegation hung over Adams' entire term and in large part, caused him to lose to Jackson four years later.

He was well known for his expertise in foreign policy due to his many years as an ambassador to various countries. He served as ambassador to Portugal and the Netherlands under President Washington, ambassador to Prussia under his father President John Adams, and as ambassador to the United Kingdom and Russia under President Madison, all of which served him well regarding foreign policy in his own presidential administration. Domestically, his main accomplishment was road building and expansion. Over all, however, he was a poor administrator.

While serving as ambassador to Prussia, Adams met the daughter of an American merchant and married her in London. She is the only First Lady to be foreign born.

After the War of 1812, Europe was faced with a recession, which led the British to offer goods to the United States at prices American manufacturers couldn't match. Americans were buying imported goods, which was causing U.S. businesses to fail because the money was going out but none was coming in. To protect industry in the northern United States from having to compete with the cheaper European imported goods, Congress passed the Tariff of 1828 to increase the price of imported European products. It was the highest protective tariff in American history, imposing a 62% tax on 92% of all imported goods, earning the nickname of "Tariff of Abominations" because of its affect on the south, which had to pay higher prices for manufactured goods the south didn't produce while facing a reduced income on sales of raw materials. The tariff reduced the importation of British goods making it difficult for the British to pay for the cotton they purchased from the south. The harmful situation continued until a lower tariff was passed in 1832 but Adams realized that signing the 1828 bill would more than likely cost him reelection, which it did.

Due to the acrimonious relationship between Adams and Andrew Jackson, members of Congress were divided regarding their loyalties and as a result, Adams was unable to accomplish much due to the opposition he faced from Congress.

When Andrew Jackson won the 1828 election, he made a point of not paying the traditional "courtesy call" to the outgoing president and as a result, Adams chose not to attend his successor's inauguration.

After leaving office, Adams became the first president to win election to the U.S. House of Representatives after serving as president. He remained a representative for the last seventeen years of his life.

His son also had a career in diplomacy and politics and established the first presidential library to honor his father after Adams died.

ANDREW JACKSON

1767 – 1845

Seventh President of the United States

Presidential term: 1829-1837. Democratic-Republican Party. Jackson was a judge, farmer, and a co-founder of the current day Democratic Party.

Life was made much more pleasant for those who lived in the executive residence when indoor plumbing was installed in the White House in 1834...a perk that was particularly appreciated when one considers the difficult personality with which the staff had to deal.

Prior to passage of the 12th Amendment regarding the electoral college, a problem arose with the prior presidential election results. Jackson ran against Adams and no majority of votes declared the winner for the sixth president of the United States so the decision went to the House of Representatives where John Quincy Adams was voted in as president by one vote - the swing vote of Henry Clay who was Speaker of the House. Adams then appointed Clay to his cabinet and Jackson irately alleged a "corrupt bargain" had been forged. He caused tremendous conflict in Adam's presidency and vowed to run again in 1828, which he did, and won.

Considered an 'outsider,' Jackson was the first non-aristocratic self-made president from outside Virginia and considered himself the true representative of the people since, prior to the electoral college, the president was the only constitutionally elected official to be elected by *all* the people of the nation. He abhorred aristocracy and began a new era in political life that ushered in a prospect of opportunity for everyone, not just the wealthy, and leaned more toward true democracy than a republic.

Jackson believed the general public should have more say in the way government was conducted and how the populace was represented. He optimistically believed if a majority was on the wrong track, the nation would eventually recognize that fact and mend it. To that end he said, *"Never for a moment believe that the great body of the citizens of any State or States can deliberately intend to do wrong. They may, under the influence of temporary excitement or misguided opinions, commit mistakes; they may be misled for a time by the suggestions of self-interest; but in a community so enlightened and patriotic as the people of the United States, argument will soon make them sensible of their errors, and when convinced, they will be ready to repair them."*

Jackson was a complicated individual whose outlook and actions were reminiscent of a person suffering a split personality. He was capable of great good when it pertained to expanding democracy and fighting economic corruption within the government, yet just as capable of evil in destroying the lives of American Indians and defending slavery.

He was best known for keeping the Union together by defeating South Carolina's attempt at secession and crushing the corrupt federal bank but his sour and revengeful attitude caused his presidency to be marred by reprehensible behavior and decisions. Jackson surrounded himself with cronies known as the "kitchen cabinet" and the nepotism in his cabinet started an unfortunate "spoils system" of rewarding party loyalists for their support. Thomas Jefferson described Jackson as *"a dangerous man unfit for president,"* and Jackson sometimes lived up to that description, even going so far as to exhibit criminal behavior.

The 'Nullification Crisis' of 1828-1832 saw southern politicians rebel against, and declare illegal, a tariff on imported European goods, which was higher than that of the northern United States and caused prices paid by southern planters to rise substantially. Congress passed a "Force Bill" and Jackson sent troops to implement the tariff as well as force South Carolina to abandon their intent to secede. A later compromise regarding the tariff relaxed tensions but it was not the last of Jackson's contentious actions.

South Carolina was assembling their own armed forces to defend themselves in their effort to secede. Jackson strongly believed that would destroy the Union and swore to crush any rebellion. Asserting that armed force on the part of

South Carolina in order to secede was treason, a showdown ensued when Jackson sent warships to the state resulting in the secessionists backing down and the state remaining in the Union. Jackson's *Proclamation to the People of South Carolina* became the precedent and blueprint on which Abraham Lincoln based his struggle to keep the nation united against secession.

The most controversial, tragic, and cold-hearted event was the Trail of Tears disaster.[1] Jackson was a devotee of 'Indian removal" and even signed a law in 1830 that allowed the president to purchase tribal land in the east and relocate Indians further west, outside U.S. state boundaries. Gold was discovered on Cherokee land in Georgia and the state wanted to take tribal land for themselves. The case went all the way to the U.S. Supreme Court, which ruled Georgia could not impose its laws upon sovereign tribal land. Jackson defiantly ignored the Supreme Court ruling but since his term was nearly over, enforcement of Jackson's demands was passed on to his successor and good friend, Martin Van Buren, and resulted in the tragic and shameful "Trail of Tears" in which many American Indians died in a forced march to their relocation site.

A states rights advocate, much of his second term was spent fighting the restructure of the federal bank, the U.S. Bank, which controlled federal deposits. Loans and payments were made to lawmakers, public officials, and private shareholders who could be useful to the bank and who acquired monetary gain from the financial institution. Jackson waged war on the corruption perpetrated by the rich and powerful elite who bent the rules in order to use the bank for their own selfish ends by vetoing the bank's recharter. By the end of his term, he had funneled enough money into various state banks that it prevented restructuring of the U.S. Bank, a result he found immensely satisfying.

Under Jackson's watch, the federal debt was paid in full for the first and only time in history. During his term in office, however, he was the target of an assassin – the first attempt on a sitting president – but the effort failed.

In retrospect, America has always been a land that forgives bad moral conduct, especially when the person they are forgiving has performed good as well, so evil can appear 'normal' to good people at a given time. Such was the case with Andrew Jackson. His tragic injustices were tolerated in light of a presidency dedicated to saving the Union and expanding democracy for the average citizen.

MARTIN VAN BUREN

1782 - 1862

Eighth President of the United States

Presidential term: 1837-1841. Democratic-Republican Party and Democratic Party. Van Buren was an attorney and key organizer of the Democratic Party. Actor Glenn Ford is a descendent of Martin Van Buren.

Economic hardship of the 1837 depression characterized his presidency and his administration was notable for its lack of anything distinguished.

Van Buren continued the dark cloud surrounding the tragic Trail of Tears begun by his predecessor and ordered 45,000 Indians to be relocated west in 1838. He sent 7,000 armed troops to march the Indians hundreds of miles by foot, resulting in the horrific deaths of over 4,000 Native Americans.

In a further demonstration of weak will, Van Buren also refused to come to the aid of Missouri Mormons who pleaded for his help against a governor who enacted an "Extermination Order" encouraging the murder of Mormons. Van Buren refused to intervene. His repeated reprehensible actions were the downfall of his political career and he was decisively defeated for reelection.

In a blow to Tenth Amendment states' rights, the Independent Treasury Act of 1840 reversed Jackson's efforts to place federal money in state banks by removing federal funds from the state banks and giving exclusive control of the money to the government.

Little of the Founders' visions were to be observed during Van Buren's tenure.

WILLIAM HENRY HARRISON

1773 – 1841

Ninth President of the United States

Presidential term: 3/04/1841 – 4/04/1841. Whig Party. Harrison was a soldier and the first president to have his picture taken but he was also the first president to die in office, only 31 days into his term.

He changed the direction of campaigns by becoming the first president to travel the country, giving out political keepsakes and the exposure it provided became a prototype for future campaigns.

His strong anti-Indian outlook caused him to spend twelve years extorting land from the Indians by any means necessary, including duress and mistreatment. It may be assumed that only his premature death prevented further harm to Native Americans in the vein of his predecessors Andrew Jackson and Martin Van Buren.

Harrison took pride in a heroic military career but it caused him to be 'macho' when he should have employed good sense. Despite extremely cold and inclement weather on his inaugural day, he chose not to wear a coat. His ego generated an inaugural address that was the longest in history, lasting nearly two hours. Then he rode in the parade without a coat as well, catching a cold that turned into pneumonia. Illness, stress, and lack of sleep resulted in his death a month later.

JOHN TYLER

1790 - 1862

Tenth President of the United States

Presidential term: 1841-1845. Whig and Democratic Parties. Tyler was a lawyer and the first Vice-President to inherit the presidency due to the death of a sitting president. No official policy was in place regarding "acting president" v. "official president" until the 25th Amendment was enacted in 1967.

Congress expected Tyler to continue the Whig agenda of President Harrison but he shocked Congress by vetoing nearly all their agendas, leaving government deadlocked. The Whigs banished him from the party and, with only one exception, the entire cabinet he inherited from Harrison, resigned. Tyler struggled with the Whigs for two years before the Whigs identified with the north and the Democrats became the party of the south.

Tyler was an advocate of states' rights. His biggest achievement while in office was the annexation of Texas in 1845. Other accomplishments included encouraging pioneers to settle unoccupied land, reorganizing the Navy, ending the Seminole War, and coming to a trade agreement with China. The town of Tyler, Texas is named after the president.

After he vetoed a tariff bill, Congress claimed he misused his presidential veto power and considered an impeachment resolution against the president for the first time in history but it failed.

After leaving office, Tyler sided with the Confederacy and endorsed secession.

JAMES POLK

1795 - 1849

Eleventh President of the United States

Presidential term: 1845-1849. Democratic Party. Polk was a lawyer and farmer. He was known for his ability to set an agenda and achieve it. During his term in office, Polk was responsible for large expansions of the nation's territory, including the purchase of 1.2 million square miles of southwest territory gained through the Treaty of Guadalupe Hidalgo.[2] [3]

In 1824, while still part of Mexico, Americans were invited via an agreement with Mexico, to settle the southwest because the Mexicans found they were unable to do so. President Tyler annexed Texas in 1845 and Mexico warned President Polk that admitting Texas as a U.S. state meant war, claiming that in the Adams-Onis Treaty of 1819, the U.S. relinquished all claims to Mexican territory. Nevertheless, Texas became a state under President Polk. A Mexican officer named Santa Anna declared himself dictator and terminated the 1824 agreement with the U.S., stripping Americans of their land, which resulted in many clashes between Texans and the Mexican Army. After Santa Anna attacked the Alamo, U.S. General Sam Houston and his troops went on to defeat Santa Anna, who eventually signed a treaty in 1836 ending the war and granting Texans their independence.

Even though the Texas Republic was annexed in late 1845 by a vote of Congress, Mexico still insisted they owned the territory and two years of fighting ensued. In exchange for $15-million dollars, the Treaty of Guadalupe Hidalgo was signed in 1848 in which Mexico ceded the territory now known as Arizona, New Mexico, California, Texas, and parts of Nevada, Utah, and Colorado. The U.S. Senate ratified the treaty on March 10, 1848 and the Mexican Senate did the same on May 19, 1848.

To the present day, however, Mexico continues to allege the U.S. "stole" their land despite the legal treaties.

The U.S. Naval Academy and the Smithsonian Institute opened during Polk's administration, ground was broken for the Washington Monument, and the first postage stamp was issued. The White House enjoyed their first refrigerator in 1845, although it was kept cold through ice rather than electricity. Nevertheless, it was a welcome addition as were the gaslights in 1848 that further eased life in the executive residence.

ZACHARY TAYLOR

1784 - 1850

Twelfth President of the United States

Presidential term: 1849-1850. Whig Party. Taylor was a soldier, an independent thinker, and his own man.

A moderate on slavery, he urged California to by-pass territorial status and vote for statehood, banning slavery. They did and southern leaders threatened to secede. Taylor said he would send the Army and hang those taking part in the rebellion against the union. The 'Compromise of 1850' temporarily postponed conflict but it also served to showcase existing discord and polarized the division between North and South, which ultimately resulted in battle. Hostilities were delayed for a decade during which time the northern states industrialized. The southern states lacked the ability to industrialize and the resulting advantage to the North proved advantageous when the Civil War broke out. President Taylor died from complications of a heat stroke while still in office before the bill passed.

MILLARD FILLMORE

1800 – 1874

Thirteenth President of the United States

Presidential term: 1850-1853. Whig, Anti-Masonic, American Party. Fillmore was a lawyer who assumed the presidency upon the death of President Taylor. He was never elected president on his own merits as he failed to gain the nomination for president after completing Taylor's term.

The Whig Party anticipated that Fillmore would unite the fractured party but division among Whig members in Congress over the slavery issue prevented that and Fillmore became the last Whig president.

Fillmore felt the best way to avoid conflict over the slavery issue was to support The Compromise of 1850, which was instituted by President Taylor. To that end, Fillmore appointed members to his cabinet that favored the compromise.

The Compromise of 1850 contained a series of five laws designed to resolve the slavery issue resulting from the Mexican-American War. The intent was to balance the individual interests of the southern slave states and the northern free states with the outcome including: 1) the admission of California to the Union as a free state; 2) payment to Texas for giving up its claim to what is now known as New Mexico, Arizona, and part of Nevada with the slavery issue being left up to the discretion of the territory; 3) slave trade halted in Washington, D.C. but the practice of slavery still condoned; 4) enforcement of a Fugitive Slave Act, and; 5) Kansas and Nebraska given the right to decide the slave issue for themselves. The Compromise of 1850 served to temporarily diffuse tensions throughout the United States but eventually the issue resulted in the Civil War.

The Fugitive Slave Act forced the return of run away slaves regardless of where they were in America. It only served to divide and anger the country further and cost Fillmore his reelection.

Fillmore proved to be an excellent problem solver with foreign policy situations as he paid close attention to problem areas and when a crisis arose where the Royal Navy fired on an American ship and Spain was holding 160 Americans captive, Fillmore and the state department resolved the emergency and avoided war.

Fillmore had a passion for reading and established the White House library when he found no books there. After leaving office, he ultimately died of complications from a stroke.

FRANKLIN PIERCE

1804 - 1869

Fourteenth President of the United States

Presidential term: 1853-1857. Democratic Party. Pierce was an attorney and an ancestor of George W. Bush on his mother's side.

Shortly before entering the White House, Pierce's son was crushed in a train derailment. Two other children died of typhus and his wife was extremely depressed and loathed politics so Pierce was reluctant to become president but the Democratic convention of 1852 reached a deadlock and Pierce appeared to be a good 'compromise' candidate because he was a Northerner who had strong sympathies for the South. He ran and won but his tenure was plagued by numerous grim occurrences.

The nation was hugely divided on the slavery issue and moving ever closer to civil war. Pierce favored expansion of slavery and tried to appease the South but it backfired and only made the threat of civil war become more imminent.

The 1854 Kansas-Nebraska Act allowed settlers in the new territories the right to decide for themselves whether or not to have slavery and the region was so divided on the issue that it nearly came to blows, which placed a dark cloud over Pierce's presidency. Criticism of this law was so great it resulted in the formation of the Republican Party in reaction against allowing slavery where it had been forbidden and the first Republican convention was held in Pittsburgh in 1856.

Further, The Ostend Manifesto was a dismal document in an already tense time in America. It was an aggressive secret document written by three diplomats on orders from U.S. Secretary of State William Marcy, which described plans to acquire Cuba from Spain by force if needed should a slave revolt spread to the South and to strengthen the Southern slavery based economy which was being criticized by the North. When the public learned of the document, Northerners were outraged because they felt certain the South was trying to expand slavery. The outcry was so great it prevented Cuba from becoming part of the United States but tremendous condemnation plagued the presidency as a result.

Pierce's largest success as president was the purchase of land in southern Arizona and southern New Mexico for a southern transcontinental rail line.

An indecisive and easily influenced politician who was not able to command or lead, Pierce's legacy views him as among the least effective presidents. A lifelong alcoholic, he died from cirrhosis of the liver while touring with his lifelong friend, novelist Nathaniel Hawthorne, after leaving office.

JAMES BUCHANAN

1791 - 1868

Fifteenth President of the United States

Presidential term: 1857-1861. Democratic Party. Buchanan was a lawyer and a Federalist who was faced with a financial crisis of a federal shortfall of revenue during his term. His administration began issuing deficit financing for the government, an unfortunate circumstance that remains to this day.

As President Pierce's minister to Britain, Buchanan played a large role in drafting the Ostend Manifesto, a secret document aimed at annexing Cuba by force if necessary in order to enhance the slave based economy of the South. Even though the document was squelched when the public learned of it, the South became even more supportive of Buchanan and he obtained the support of every one of the slave states in the 1856 presidential election.

As a moderate, Buchanan did little to take control of the increasing path toward civil war over the slavery and secession issues. The South was his base so he made it clear that his presidency would support a policy of nonintervention with the existing slave states.

Additionally, Buchanan enforced the Fugitive Slave Act and approved of the Kansas proslavery constitution, thereby igniting the fire toward civil war.

Shortly after taking office, the U.S. Supreme Court issued the Dred Scott Decision, which declared slaves and their descendents to be "property" and not citizens and that government had no right to deprive white slave owners of their "property." That decision inflamed the nation and further divided the North and South.

After the hanging of abolitionist John Brown at Harper's Ferry, Virginia, any hope of peaceful compromise evaporated.

The final straw for the Buchanan presidency occurred when he did nothing as southern states seceded from the union to form their own "Confederate States of America." Buchanan declared the secessions illegal but also declared any war effort to stop them, illegal as well. His lack of action directly led to the Civil War

Southern delegates walked out of the 1860 Democratic convention and started their own convention, which resulted in <u>two</u> opposing Democratic candidates and the secession of South Carolina. That situation formed the perfect climate for Republican Abraham Lincoln to win the election.

History views Buchanan's failure to deal with the secession issue as one of the greatest mistakes any president has made and ranks him as one of the worst presidents in American history.

ABRAHAM LINCOLN

1809 - 1865

Sixteenth President of the United States

Presidential term: 1861-1865. Whig Party, Republican Party. Lincoln was an attorney. Known as the president that freed the slaves, the actual issue for Lincoln was preventing any secession from the Union. Animosity created by his controversial and illegal actions divided the country instead of uniting it. From Lincoln's presidency forward, the form of government forever changed from a states' rights republic to an all-encompassing centralized government empire.

Lincoln's rise from abject poverty to become President of the United States is legendary. His assassination ensured his place in history as a martyr but history has been distorted and rewritten in order to accomplish that objective. The romanticized account to which most Americans are taught and exposed is regrettably void of accurate detail and the false imprint of his legend is so steadfast that anyone who attempts to shine the light of truth on the matter is nearly always denounced as being unpatriotic.

From the moment Lincoln entered politics until the day of his death, he was fixated on a single agenda - a centralized government with 'subsidies that benefited special interest, which in today's terminology is known as 'corporate welfare.' His vision embodied the very reason America pulled away from England's corruption to form a better alliance. This curriculum of tariffs, a national bank, and subsidized 'internal improvement' projects became known as the 'American System'[4] in Lincoln's time and was the central theme of the Republican Party. As an Illinois state representative, Lincoln was successful in convincing the legislature to appropriate $12-million for "improvement projects" that not only failed, the crushing debt that resulted crippled the state budget for years to come. Undaunted by the dismal failure of corporate welfare in his home state and uncaring about the hardship it caused the citizens of Illinois, Lincoln went on to relentlessly push the same agenda as president.

He made no bones about the fact slavery[5] was *not* the focus of his administration, suppressing Southern secession in an effort to force the states to remain part of the Union for economic reasons, was. The myth was perpetrated that Lincoln 'saved' the Union but his agenda was realized only through military force and he eliminated states' rights in the process.

The Founding Fathers found abuses by England's King George III so extreme, that it justified secession of the colonies from England. Sadly, Lincoln followed in the king's footsteps with the same horrendous deeds in order to accomplish his own self-serving agenda. Ultimately, citizens were under siege at the hands of their own president, government, and armed military.

The Declaration of Independence was the solid foundation of states' rights and the most important defense against the tyranny of centralized government power. The document itself was a declaration of secession from England and its language is clear that the right of any U.S. state to secede from the Union was endowed by the Declaration of Independence. Lincoln didn't see it that way, however, and took unorthodox and even tyrannical action to put a stop to secession.

The South relied heavily on Northern trade but huge and unfair tariffs were imposed on them in order to trade with the North. While the tariffs fueled a healthy economy for the North, it created severe hardship and animosity in the South, so they felt they should secede for economic reasons to form their own government and trade with Europe instead. That would have negatively impacted on the North so Lincoln was fixated on one goal - preventing the secession of the South.

The guidelines of the Founding Fathers and the true history that the nation was formed on the concept of states' rights always got in the way of those, like Lincoln, who advocated a powerful centralized government instead so they simply invented a new but very erroneous theory and rewrote history to suit their own political agendas. Daniel Webster fabricated the notion that the federal government existed first and then it created the states. Lincoln fully embraced that 'spectacular lie'[6][7] and made it the center piece of his justification for denying secession to the southern states and initiated a war to establish his point. By forcing the states to remain in the Union at gunpoint, he totally changed the meaning of the Constitution from states' rights to centralized government, thereby effectively eliminating the powers instituted in the Tenth Amendment and establishing new precedents. In so doing, Lincoln's administration forever changed the course of government.

A majority of political leaders as well as the public, viewed peaceful secession for the southern states as their inherent right, but Lincoln felt anyone who disagreed with him was a traitor. On April 27, 1861, only months after taking office, he illegally suspended habeas corpus (due process)[8] and ordered federal soldiers to arrest political leaders who were never allowed to even debate the issue of secession in the legislature. He imposed martial law and military occupation, imprisoned anyone that criticized his policies, destroyed dozens of newspaper offices that opposed his war policy, sent troops to voting places to suppress free elections, deprived citizens of their constitutional rights, and even passed the "Indemnity Act of 1863" which placed the president above the law and made him the ultimate authority of the land. Suspension of the Bill of Rights and the writ of habeas corpus continued for the remainder of his administration and elimination of civil liberties created a fear within the public that silenced any further contemplation about secession or criticism of the president's policies.

Lincoln's actions so infuriated the public that on the eve of the Civil War he had to take his train journey to the Capitol under the cover of darkness where he was smuggled from one train station to another in order to avoid feared assassination attempts.

He was determined to start a war to end states' rights and send a strong message to states that wanted to secede so he manipulated the South into firing the first shot when he sent a naval force to Fort Sumter,[9] South Carolina under the guise of sending food and supplies to southern troops. War ships were also sent, however, and Lincoln fully understood the South would fire on them because they would feel they were under assault. If the South fired first, it would make Lincoln look like the hero who was sending supplies and was unfairly fired upon. His plan worked and he launched a war without the consent of Congress. The Founders would never have imagined an American president would send an invading army to kill citizens of his own country in order to destroy the very right of secession the Declaration of Independence established, but Lincoln did just that.

During the Civil War, he seized powers no other president dared to even consider and micro-managed every aspect of the war. He was quite clear that he wanted the South to live in a state of terror as a means of obtaining his goal and was even known to sleep at the telegraph office so he could get the latest details of General Sherman and General Sheridan's diabolical marches through the South as they pillaged, plundered, raped, and murdered unarmed women, children, old men, and slaves and burned entire towns to the ground. It is certain he knew full well what was going on and made no attempt to stop it. There was talk at the time of 'war crimes' but only the losing side is on the judicial end of justice and Lincoln was the dubious 'winner' so a completely ruined and destitute South was left with no recourse.

Lincoln closed 3500 miles of Confederate coastline along with twelve major ports in order to prevent the passage of supplies and goods to Confederate troops, captured 18,000 blockade runners and Confederate sympathizers and put them in prison without benefit of due process. The war was nearly over when he authorized General Sherman, a cruel man who enjoyed his murderous work, to capture and burn Atlanta, targeting civilians and infrastructure and even using freed slaves to shore up his troops. Lincoln had a morbid fascination with details from the battlefield, especially with General Sherman's assault on Atlanta which resulted in an unnecessarily huge death toll. General Lee surrendered on April 9, 1865, finally ending the Civil War and Lincoln flaunted victory by making a special trip to Richmond, Virginia to make a public display of sitting in defeated Confederate President Jefferson Davis' desk, thereby sending a clear message that Lincoln ruled the entire land.

The 'Emancipation Proclamation'[10][11][12] of 1862 addressed only southern slaves and in actuality, freed none of them. While it shifted the focus from preventing secession to the slavery issue, it was, however, the beginning of the end of slavery.

Passage of the 'Emancipation Proclamation' and the 13th Amendment, which abolished slavery, were viewed as highlights of Lincoln's presidency but he considered them as only 'political maneuvers' to weaken rebellion by southern slave-owners by destroying their economic base and to sidestep the issue of a desperate military situation. In Lincoln's view, if the slaves were freed, the plantation owners would lose their free labor, their economy would diminish, and there would be fewer males to fight the war in the South. Although history has elevated Lincoln to near sainthood, the dark side of his personality inflicted great premeditated and unnecessary harm on the American people.

Imposing the first federal income tax in American history did nothing to endear Lincoln further. It forced every citizen to forever have direct contact with the federal government in direct violation of the states' rights vision of the Founding Fathers. The biggest cost of the Civil War was the annihilation of states' rights in which the federal government became the master, rather than the servant, of the people. Federal taxation nailed down the final plank in that effort.

Due to public sentiment, Lincoln had little chance for reelection but crucial Union victories wound up giving him the election after all. Less than three months after taking office for the second time, he was dead.

So many of Lincoln's actions during his time in office were unconscionable and the country was ruled by fear. He changed a states rights' nation into a centralized government, circumvented the U.S. Constitution to achieve his own agendas, and began a destructive downward spiral away from the intent of the Founders, which began an escalation through future administrations that has culminated in the crisis America faces in the 21st Century. He shifted the national power structure, changed the office of president, and circumvented the Constitution itself in ways that can never be repaired.

To some, Lincoln led the nation as few could, but to others the thought of another single day in office was too frightening for many to even imagine. Is it possible Lincoln's brutal destruction of civil liberties and his use of military force to make sure his demands were met, fueled a fear so intense in John Wilkes Booth that, in his mind, he was saving the country more despair by killing Lincoln to prevent another four or more years in office? Nevertheless, one of the darkest periods of American history has been rewritten in a biased manner that ignores truth and elevates a tyrant to sainthood.

ANDREW JOHNSON

1808 - 1875

Seventeenth President of the United States

Presidential term: 1865-1869. No party affiliation during presidential term. Johnson was a tailor who ascended to the presidency upon the assassination of President Lincoln.

His main function as president was post-Civil War reconstruction, a daunting task made more difficult by Johnson's rigid personality, limited intellect, and Lincoln's Republicans. He found himself simply overwhelmed and largely but unfairly considered a failure as president.

Johnson was constantly at war with congress, which was mainly made up of post-Lincoln administration Republicans. In a blatant attempt to further abolish states' rights, congress gave itself unheard of power to intrude upon the civil status of states, imposing the federal government into decisions that were constitutionally given to the states by the Tenth Amendment. When white supremacists were placed in local government positions, it basically relegated blacks to the status of second class citizens and encouraged a reign of terror by the Ku Klux Klan that continued for decades. Every attempt to assist southern rebuilding by President Johnson was blocked by Lincoln's Republicans so history deemed Johnson's Reconstruction efforts to build an interracial democracy out the ruins of slavery to be noble but flawed and considered his efforts to be a failure, totally ignoring historical facts to the contrary.

Lincoln's Republicans generated as many complaints against Johnson as possible over his reconstruction policies in their effort to centralize government. After Johnson vetoed the unlawful congressional 1866 Civil Rights Bill, the First Reconstruction Act, and the expansion of authority of the Freedman's Bureau, Congress usurped the president's executive power authority and brought impeachment proceedings against him.

Johnson became the first president to be impeached by the U.S. House of Representatives but acquitted when the Senate vote fell short by a single ballot. Events during Johnson's presidency validated how successful Lincoln was in destroying the Founding Father's outline for the Office of President and how pervasively Lincoln circumvented the Constitution and changed the fundamental framework of the Founders.

Given the opposition he faced from Lincoln's Republicans and their obsession with rewriting Constitutional powers, his only two real accomplishments while in office were the purchase of Alaska from Russia, which was viewed as vital to the national security and the removal of French forces from Mexico.

Johnson left office an understandably bitter man and likely one of the most hampered by Congress and Lincoln's Republicans in his ability to do his job.

ULYSSES S. GRANT

1822 - 1885

Eighteenth President of the United States

Presidential term: 1869-1877. Republican Party. Grant was a soldier of exceptional repute. His military ability was such that President Lincoln placed him in command of the entire Union Army in 1864 and Grant brought victory to the North and an end to the Civil War.

His reputation as a 'common man' who rose to military hero and ended the war, propelled him into the White House but he found himself in over his head in politics where he lacked competent leadership skills the nation sorely needed following the Civil War. Grant himself admitted he was not suited to be president and his passive nature and lack of ambition eventually proved him right, as history ranks him as a presidential failure.

While serving as commanding general of the army under President Andrew Johnson, Grant observed the president at total odds with congress over his efforts at post-Civil War Reconstruction. Congress intruded upon states rights by putting white supremacists in positions of local government, which assured renewed suppression of southern blacks. Northern Republicans used ex-slaves as pawns during Reconstruction to further plunder the south in exchange for insignificant bribes, which so incensed southern residents against the ex-slaves that it resulted in the formation of the Ku Klux Klan. Grant lacked the personality or ability to put an end to that situation when he became president.

Just prior to becoming president, Grant contributed to further destruction of the Founder's principles when he assisted greedy Republican 'carpetbaggers' in the post-war south. The railroad was viewed as an economic 'gold mine' for land grabbing Republicans and Grant helped implement their scheme by instructing General Sherman to conduct a campaign of 'ethnic genocide' against the Plains Indians so a government subsidized railroad could be built through their land. In just a few short years, the ideal of the Founding Fathers to protect the civil rights of the nation's residents had been reduced to an imperialistic power grab that was willing to trample civil liberties and the Constitution to obtain their objective.

A concern of the Founders was that, should the new nation stray from the Constitution, the result would be corruption due to political bribes. As president, Grant continued in the Lincoln Republican mind set to further abolish states' rights and expand centralized government. By circumventing the Constitution, Republicans guaranteed corruption and the Founder's fears were realized when Grant appointed cronies and campaign contributors to his cabinet who proved to be corrupt con artists and brought dishonor to Grant's presidency.

Grant's administration was riddled with scandals including terrorization of southern blacks, rebellion by Indians who were victimized by their enemies, a changing economy that brought social conflict and left nearly all the nation's wealth in the hands of only 1% of America's inhabitants, his vice president who accepted railroad stock, his secretary of war who resigned after defrauding the Indian Agency, his treasury secretary who was connected to a tax swindle, and even the indictment of his private secretary who was part of the Whiskey Ring, a stock swindle scam. Grant even conceived the term 'lobbyist' to describe the men who hung around hotel lobbies waiting to bribe congressional members. A basically honest man, Grant simply was unable to see evil in those around him and made the situation worse by remaining loyal to those that betrayed his trust rather than taking a strong stand to halt it. Federal employment to favored people further inflated a centralized government and began the large federal job market we have today.

Grant bestowed amnesty to Confederate leaders, supervised the ratification of the 15th Amendment, which established equality in voting rights, and created Yellowstone National Park, America's first national park. The depression of

1873 gave Democrats control of congress the following year and greatly hampered the president's ability to accomplish much more.

After leaving office, Grant proved to be so lacking in economic issues that a friend even swindled him out of his last personal funds and Grant became poverty-stricken. Congress viewed that as unacceptable and embarrassing to the government so a bill was passed granting the president a pension for the first time, a practice that continues to the present.

RUTHERFORD B. HAYES

1822 - 1893

Nineteenth President of the United States

Presidential term: 1877-1881. Republican Party. Hayes was a lawyer whose election was marked by the need to form a special electoral commission to decide who would take office. Democrats won the popular vote but Republicans won the electoral votes. Hayes was chosen upon his promise to withdraw Union troops from the South and end Reconstruction, as well as appoint one southerner to his cabinet.

An honest man, Hayes' main focus in office was reform, which wound up costing him his power base. He worked endlessly to reverse Grant's government patronage and institute a procedure of merit-based appointments instead. Sound fiscal policies were put in place by the president and he worked toward bettering education for black Americans.

His administration was marred by a railroad strike in 1877 when violent riots broke out all across the country. Hayes dispatched troops who fired on members of the labor dispute for the first time in U.S. history, resulting in 70 deaths.

The President signed a bill in 1879 that allowed females to argue cases before the U.S. Supreme Court for the first time.

Hayes was the first president to have a phone, which was installed in 1879 with '1' designated as the White House's number. A delighted staff received the first typewriters in 1880. Hayes' wife was the first spouse to be called the "First Lady," as well as the first wife to have obtained a college degree but she hampered the president's popularity by refusing to serve liquor in the White House. President Hayes and the First Lady were the first White House occupants to begin the custom of an Easter Egg Roll on the White House lawn.

Keeping his campaign pledge to not run for a second term as president, Hayes declined to run for reelection and instead, served on the Board of Trustees of Ohio State University, which he helped to found. He spent 12 years in that post until he died from a heart attack.

JAMES GARFIELD

1831 - 1881

Twentieth President of the United States

Presidential term: 3/04/1881 – 9/19/1881. Republican Party. Garfield was a lawyer, educator, and minister.

He attended the 1880 Republican Convention to campaign for another candidate but the convention became deadlocked and Republicans nominated Garfield instead as a candidate with little chance to win. He did win, however, and went on to conduct his presidency as a moderate.

Like former president Grant, Garfield was an advocate of the political patronage system and was excessive in its application, canceling out former president Hayes' good efforts to appoint office holders according to merit rather than by the crony and payback system.

Garfield was only the second president to be assassinated and was shot after only four months in office. His short tenure gave him virtually no time to accomplish anything of distinction. The murderer was a disgruntled man who failed to receive a political appointment and shot Garfield when he was on his way to Williams College where he had studied for the ministry. Ironically, Abraham Lincoln's son, Robert, was walking with the president when he was shot.

CHESTER ARTHUR

1829 - 1886

Twenty-first President of the United States

Presidential term: 1881-1885. Republican Party. Arthur was an attorney who became president upon the assassination of President Garfield.

Prior to his presidency, Arthur got involved with Senator Roscoe Conkling in building a corrupt Republican political machine. Conkling rewarded him by appointing Arthur as New York Customs Collector where he was in charge of a major portion of the country's tariff revenue. The office was ripe for corruption and theft but Arthur did his best to achieve a balance between the New York bosses and doing his job independently. Nevertheless, the agency gave government a black eye so President Hayes removed Arthur from his post.

A snappy dresser, he earned the nickname of "Elegant Arthur." His penchant for cronyism in rewarding his friends with appointments to office saw him awarding more offices than the president should have and caused many to distrust his intentions.

His main presidential achievements were in the arena of civil service reform where he was known as "the father of civil service." He established a bi-partisan civil service commission and enacted the first immigration laws.

The 1882 Chinese Exclusion Act was a federal law that allowed the U.S. to suspend immigration. The western gold rush and the prospect of building tracks for the railroads brought many Chinese to the U.S. Fear that the Chinese would stake claim to the gold shamefully caused a ban on Chinese immigration that lasted sixty years until it was repealed in 1943.

The Pendleton Civil Service Reform Act of 1883 was a federal law that focused on granting federal jobs based on experience rather than political payback. It created a 'merit system' to replace the 'spoils system' of awarding jobs to friends and family and passed as a result of a disgruntled office seeker who assassinated President James Garfield when he was denied a civil service position. Due to his fondness of the crony reward system for federal jobs, Arthur was reluctant to sign the bill.

The Civil Rights Cases of 1883 combined several racial discrimination charges by blacks. The U.S. Supreme Court ruled the federal government had no jurisdiction to regulate state laws, which opened the door to widespread segregation that lasted until the 1960s civil rights movement.

Arthur entered office widely distrusted but despite controversial events during his presidency he still left as a respected leader.

GROVER CLEVELAND

1837 - 1908

Twenty-second President of the United States

Presidential term: 1885-1889. Democratic Party. Cleveland was an attorney and the only president to serve two non-consecutive terms. He was the 22nd president as well as the 24th president.

Known for his honesty, he fought corruption, disliked elitist behavior, taxes, and inflationary policies. In protection of states' rights, he vetoed hundreds of bills that attempted to confer more power to a centralized government. He was a guardian of the national interest and ran an efficient government with little tolerance for government abuse. His biggest failing was his insensitivity to working people, which caused his popularity to decline during his second administration.

During his first term in office, Cleveland lowered tariffs, vetoed excessive Veteran's pension legislation, and extended the merit system through civil service reform. He was also proud to preside over the dedication of the Statue of Liberty.

The Panic of 1893 was one of the worst depressions in U.S. history but an event Cleveland was powerless to avoid. In an effort to diminish the effects of the depression Cleveland imposed the gold standard but when reserves reached perilously low levels he was forced to purchase more gold from big business, thus allowing corporations to bail out the government and increasing the power of big business at the expense of the working class.

The 1894 American Railway Union went on strike to protest wage cuts and federal troops were dispatched to suppress the strikers. The 'Interstate Commerce Act' was signed into law as the first attempt by the federal government to regulate the railroads in order to ensure fair rates, eliminate rate discrimination, and regulate other various aspects of carriers until it was disbanded in 1995.

That same year, a large protest march demonstrated the working people's anger over government's failure to protect them with legislation.

Cleveland loved the ladies and admitted to fathering an illegitimate child. That didn't stop him from marrying while in office, however. In 1886, Cleveland became the second sitting president to marry and the first to marry in the White House.

BENJAMIN HARRISON

1833 - 1901

Twenty-third President of the United States

Presidential term: 1889-1893. Republican Party. Harrison was a lawyer, the great-grandson of a Declaration of Independence signer, and the grandson of former President William Henry Harrison. They are the only grandfather/grandson pair of presidents.

He was the first president to travel across the United States entirely by train and the first to attend a baseball game. In 1891, electric lights replaced gaslights in the White House.

Harrison advanced the alliance between big business and the Republican party by promoting high tariffs but growing hostility toward the high tariffs and big business intensified support for the Populist party and the labor movement and made Republicans so unpopular that it gave Democrats control of the Congress in 1890 and led to bringing Democrat Grover Cleveland back into the White House in 1893.

In 1890, the McKinley Tariff Act was passed to set the tariff rate but it also established the practice of 'bartering' with the opposite political party for passage of bills that they wanted in exchange for supporting the requested bill. The tariff was harmful to the American public because it raised the price of purchased goods and forced imported goods to be raised to the higher price of local goods and by increasing the cost of goods, it forced an increase in wages which drove up the price of manufactured products and labor and an unending vicious cycle ensued. The tariff was doomed to failure and cost Harrison reelection.

A dark period during Harrison's term was the 1890 Wounded Knee Massacre. U.S. troops were ordered to put the Sioux Indians on a train for relocation to Nebraska, an order the Indians didn't fight. They turned themselves in but the troops were ordered to confiscate their firearms. A deaf Native

American didn't understand the order and demanded payment for his rifle if the troops were going to take it. Chaos resulted and led to the killing of 146 Lakota Sioux Indians.

The Sherman Anti-Trust Act of 1890 was the first federal act of its kind to limit monopolies in order to protect trade and commerce but it wasn't widely used until the administration of Teddy Roosevelt.

Harrison was renowned for his large federal spending but he actually had little impact on wide ranging policies during his term as president. His primary accomplishments included admitting six states to the Union, bringing Teddy Roosevelt into his administration as civil service commissioner, commencing modernization of the Navy, and making foreign policy a central focus of his administration.

GROVER CLEVELAND

1837 - 1908

Twenty-fourth President of the United States

Presidential term: 1893-1897. Democratic Party. Cleveland was an attorney who resumed living in the White House in 1893 after the presidency of Benjamin Harrison separated his two terms.

Cleveland continued Harrison's efforts to modernize the U.S. Navy.

The president intervened in the 1894 Pullman Strike in an attempt to keep the railroads moving but he tremendously angered labor unions when he obtained an injunction to prevent the shut down of the railroads and sent in troops when strikers refused to obey the injunction.

The economic depression in 1893 saw the stock market fall but Cleveland was able to maintain the gold reserve with help from Wall Street, which only served to inject big business further into government at the expense of the working class.

While still in office he underwent secret surgery to cure cancer of his upper palate.

WILLIAM McKINLEY

1843 - 1901

Twenty-fifth President of the United States

Presidential term: 1897-1901. Republican Party. McKinley was a lawyer who, as Governor of Ohio, left the office early to run for president. He was the first presidential candidate to use advertising to win an election, thereby revolutionizing campaign practices. Mt. McKinley, Alaska is named after him.

Following in the footsteps of Lincoln Republicans, the McKinley Tariff was detrimental to the American people because it catered to big business to the detriment of the working class and forced an imperialistic stance upon the nation. The focal point of his administration was keeping tariffs high on imports to maintain prosperity but inflation and high prices only served to make the average American poorer.

Civil service weakened during McKinley's administration when the protection of the merit system and competitive exams were replaced by his secretary of war to allow thousands to enter civil service without benefit of that process. It displaced many who had toiled under the original system for years.

The Republic of Hawaii was annexed through the use of a joint resolution that provided for the U.S. to assume the $4-million Hawaiian debt and required that Chinese immigration from Hawaii to the mainland would be prohibited.

The brief Spanish-American War resulted in the acquisition of the Philippines, Guam, and Puerto Rico, which ultimately involved the U.S. in further military intervention in World War I. McKinley was the first president to have phone and telegraph services to keep him in touch with battlefield personnel during the Spanish-American War and during this time he violated the First Amendment by censoring news regarding the conflict.

McKinley was assassinated on September 14, 1901 by Leon Czolgosz, a child of Polish immigrants who felt the rich victimized the poor as a result of government's structure and he had to take matters into his own hands for the good of the common man. He was not affiliated with any insurgency organization and acted on his own when he went through a receiving line at an exhibition the president attended and shot him point blank. Czolgosz was electrocuted a month later at Auburn Prison in New York and buried on the prison grounds.

THEODORE ROOSEVELT

1858 - 1919

Twenty-sixth President of the United States

Presidential term: 1901- 1909. Republican Party. Roosevelt was an author, conservationist, historian, and civil servant. He was an extremely fascinating, dynamic, and active man with many varied interests so when the news came that President McKinley had died and Roosevelt was now president, it shouldn't have been surprising that he was climbing a mountain and had to be rushed back to the seat of government.

As a child, he idealized his father who held a deep love of humanity and greatly influenced his son. Roosevelt's future decisions were always compared to the measuring stick of his father. He also suffered from life threatening asthma, which motivated him to push the limits of physical activity in order to develop his body and fight the disease.

When his first wife died after giving birth to their only daughter, Roosevelt was so devastated that he left the child with his sister and moved to the Dakota territory to become a cowboy. A bad winter wiped out his herd and he returned to New York shortly thereafter where he remarried, brought his daughter into his new marriage, and subsequently had five more children.

In 1902, shortly after Roosevelt took office, he officially named the executive residence the "White House" and added the West Wing making the White House a separate residence from official offices. In 1909, the first location for the Oval Office was added in the center of the West Wing's South side. During a parade, he became the first president to take a public automobile ride as well as the first president to fly in an airplane.

Roosevelt was best known for commanding the 'Rough Riders,' of the 1st U.S. Voluntary Calvary Regiment during the Spanish-American War where he led his men in a charge during the battle of San Juan in Cuba. When he returned to the United States he did so as a war hero and easily won election to the presidency.

A dynamic leader, Roosevelt forged a new and more democratic social arrangement. He was a progressive liberal who worked on behalf of labor, attacked corruption, reformed civil service, advocated on behalf of the common man, and made America a world power. His famous 'Square Deal' policy promised a fair shake for the average citizen.

Industry was unregulated when he took office and the sheer wealth and arrogance of big business had divided America. The working class was poor and angry and Roosevelt knew he had to begin to regulate free enterprise. He was the first president to actively intervene on behalf of the average citizen against big corporate businesses and his trust-busting efforts began breaking up the monopolies of the country's most powerful entities. Congress subsequently created the Department of Commerce and Labor to regulate and scrutinize corporate America.

A devoted conservationist, Roosevelt established numerous irrigation projects through the Newlands Act of 1902 and the first National Bird Preserve, which eventually became the Wildlife Refuge system. He went on to create the U.S. Forest Service and numerous national parks including the Grand Canyon National Park. The president negotiated an end to the United Mine Workers strike in 1902 as well, which put him in good graces with labor.

He felt it was the duty of civilized nations to help underdeveloped countries so in that vein he sent medical services, the Army Corps of Engineers, and American teachers to assist poor countries. Additionally, he increased the size of the U.S. Navy to elevate America's presence in the eyes of other nations.

During Roosevelt's first term the Hepburn Act was passed, which granted the Interstate Commerce Commission permission to oversee the railroads. Also during this time the Food and Drug Act as well as the Meat Inspection Act were put in place and he became an early defender of womens' rights. The president encouraged a revolution in Panama that gave the nation their independence and obtained the Panama Canal for America, which became one of his most significant, if not controversial, achievements.

In 1906, he became the first American to be awarded the Nobel Peace Prize for his part in negotiating peace in the Russo-Japanese War. Along with those negotiations he also arbitrated a dispute between France and Germany over Morocco. Both actions contributed to the avoidance of a world war. Roosevelt stressed character as well as policy during his presidency and was well loved by Americans so he easily won reelection.

Charles Bonaparte, grandson of France's infamous Napoleon Bonaparte, founded the FBI in 1908 while serving as Roosevelt's Attorney General.

Early in his administration Roosevelt impulsively made a promise he later regretted that he would not seek a third term. His hand picked protégé, William Howard Taft, was elected to succeed him. Roosevelt became so infuriated with Taft's refusal to stand up to corporate power that in 1912 he defiantly formed and ran on his own Progressive 'Bull Moose' ticket when the Republicans declined to nominate him for president. He lost but so many voters were pulled to his ticket that it split the Republican vote and the presidency went to a Democrat, Woodrow Wilson.

When Roosevelt died in his sleep in 1919, Woodrow Wilson's Vice President Thomas Marshall remarked, "*Death had to take Roosevelt sleeping, for if he had been awake, there would have been a fight.*" Roosevelt was posthumously awarded the Medal of Honor for his charge up a San Juan hill during the Spanish-American War, the first president to receive that honor. His legacy is forever ensured, however, in the form of a stuffed toy animal … the Teddy Bear.

WILLIAM HOWARD TAFT

1857 - 1930

Twenty-seventh President of the United States

Presidential term: 1909-1913. Republican Party. Taft was a lawyer who disliked politics intensely and had no ambition to become president.

Prior to his presidency Taft was appointed civil governor of the Philippines, an American possession. Under his guidance as governor the troubled region realized peace. When Teddy Roosevelt became president he appointed Taft as his secretary of war and Taft became one of the president's closest advisors.

Taft's lifelong obsession was with the judicial system so when he became president much of his tenure was spent applying the law to all aspects of his presidency. He greatly favored anything judicial and felt the judicial system was superior to everything else. He granted more power to federal courts and the U.S. Supreme Court than other administrations.

Although he was more conservative than his mentor, Taft nevertheless carried on Roosevelt's trustbusting, support of labor, and conservation efforts. Numerous anti-trust suits were filed at Taft's behest, even against U.S. Steel, the country's largest corporation. He supported passage of the 16th Amendment to create a federal income tax and the 17th Amendment, which allowed election of senators by the people rather than by legislative appointment. The parcel post system was established during his tenure and the president expanded the civil service system and strengthened the Interstate Commerce Commission.

Due to his lack of foresight and understanding of human nature, Taft alienated many factions during his time in office which caused a major split within the GOP that alienated even his close friend Theodore Roosevelt and contributed to Roosevelt forming his own Bull Moose Party, which effectively split the vote and gave the 28th presidency to a Democrat, Woodrow Wilson.

After leaving office, his lifelong dream was realized when U.S. Supreme Court Justice Edward White died and President Harding appointed Taft as Chief Justice. He is the only president to have led both the executive and judicial branches of government and the first president to be buried in Arlington National Cemetery.

(THOMAS) WOODROW WILSON

1856 - 1924

Twenty-eighth President of the United States

Presidential term: 1913-1921. Democratic Party. Wilson was an Academic and the only president to earn a Ph.D. He worked briefly as an attorney. He was the first sitting president to attend a World Series baseball game and throw out the first ball.

He was an intellectual who viewed himself as superior to others and was known as a reformer and a visionary. Disappointingly, he allowed himself to be overly influenced by Socialist advisors. During his administration he made progress in achieving peace and was awarded the Nobel Peace Prize in 1919 for those efforts.

Nevertheless, Wilson unwisely allowed Edward House, who was a Socialist activist that embraced the radical Karl Marx philosophy, to become a close advisor who yielded considerable influence upon the president's decisions to the detriment of the nation. He was a key player in secret meetings of bankers and politicians who created the Federal Reserve in 1913. The Reserve shifted the power to create money from the U.S. government to a private group of bankers, thereby becoming the largest producers of debt worldwide.

Wilson discussed the New World Order theory in his 'Fourteen Points' speech in 1918, which was a Karl Marx/ Socialist philosophy outlined by House and endorsed by Wilson. House later packed the reorganized Council of Foreign Affairs with Socialists who promoted a One World Government and hand picked many leaders.

During his administration, Wilson signed the 1914 Clayton Antitrust Act, which set an 8-hour work day for railroad workers and later for all labor and passed laws to stop child labor exploitation, created the Public Utilities Commission, encouraged passage of the Federal Trade Commission, which tremendously helped stop unfair trade practices, promoted funding of public highways, implemented the 1916 Federal Farm Loan Act, passed the Underwood Act, which lowered tariffs that big business had kept high for years, and introduced the first graduated income tax.

Wilson promoted labor union growth but the country suffered an immense number of strikes, race riots broke out, and a healthy economy plunged into financial depression.

War broke out in Europe in 1914 and because Wilson remembered the horror of the Civil War as a child, he wanted to avoid conflict if at all possible. By 1917, he could no longer keep America out of the war when German submarines resumed unrestricted submarine warfare and threatened American submarines. Wilson pushed through the Selective Service Act of 1917, which instituted the first military draft, took over control of the railroads, and suppressed anti-war protests.

Because Wilson feared extensive public dissension that might threaten victory during the war, the president declared it 'necessary' to 'save' Americans with the Espionage Act of 1917. He prosecuted over 2,000 Americans, especially those he labeled 'hyphenated Americans' simply because they protested the war, imprisoned newspaper editors for simply speaking out against the war, banned mailing of publications the president deemed in violation of the Act, censored news by instructing the postal service to not allow 75 newspapers to mail their publications, intimidated other newspapers into not writing anything about the war by threatening to not allow them access to the postal system as well, and in general, used the law to abuse his presidential power and violate the Constitution.

After years of public demonstrations and severe abuse of women suffragists in the justice system, the bad publicity it brought Wilson's administration caused the president to reluctantly support the 19th Amendment giving women the right to vote in 1920.

His biggest liability was his absolute inflexible nature and inability to compromise. After the war, he longed to see the U.S. join the League of Nations as the high point of his administration but stubborn defiance against suggestions by opponents defeated that goal. His rigidity was so extreme that it was even attributed to possible brain damage due to a stroke.

Two years before the end of his administration the president suffered a serious stroke that left him almost totally incapacitated. His condition was kept secret from the public and his wife Edith, for all intent and purpose, ran the government until the end of his term.

WARREN HARDING

1865 - 1923

Twenty-ninth President of the United States

Presidential term: 1921-1923. Republican Party. Harding was a newspaper publisher.

Despite his popularity, history ranks him as one of the least successful presidents and even Harding himself admitted he was in over his head. His wife was the strong one of the two and was a determined ambitious woman who was credited with pushing Harding into the presidency. His presidential campaign was the first to receive widespread publicity and incorporate Hollywood and Broadway stars to attract votes. His was also the first election to include the women's vote.

Harding established the Bureau of Veteran's Affairs, later known as the Department of Veteran's Affairs but the most notable event of his administration was the end of World War I.

His administration was plagued by scandals, a fact Harding found especially unsettling since most of his administration was made up of personal friends. While the president played no part in corruption of his organization, he did have his own scandals. He had more than one extra-martial affair and one resulted in the birth of a daughter for which he paid lavish child support. To avoid scandal during his campaign, the GOP sent Carrie Phillips, who had a 15-year affair with Harding, on a trip to Japan, paid her $50,000, and regular monthly stipends after that. Harding was so distressed at all the scandals in his administration that he suffered a heart attack and died before his term was up.

CALVIN COOLIDGE

1872 - 1933

Thirtieth President of the United States

Presidential term: 1923-1929. Republican Party. Coolidge was a lawyer and the only president born on the 4th of July. He became president upon the death of Warren Harding and restored confidence in the White House after the scandals of the previous administration.

A quiet and serious laid-back personality, Coolidge nevertheless was popular with the middle class and gained approval with his reduction of federal government. Because he inherited the presidency, he decided he should carry on Harding's goals until the next election, including restriction of immigration and arbitration of coal strikes. He signed into law the Revenue Act of 1924, which decreased personal income tax rates.

Shortly before his second term, Coolidge's son died and the president became very withdrawn.

The 'Roaring 20s' were in full swing with healthy economic growth. Coolidge reduced federal spending, paid off a good portion of the federal debt, and signed a bill giving Native Americans full citizenship. He was not strong on foreign policy and avoided doing much in that vein.

The inauguration of Coolidge was the first to be broadcast on radio and he was the first president to appear in a sound film. The first electric refrigerator was installed in 1926, followed by a clothes washer in 1929.

HERBERT HOOVER

1874 - 1964

Thirty-first President of the United States

Presidential term: 1929-1933. Republican Party. Hoover was a mining engineer and a humanitarian. A central theme of his administration was to promote economic modernization but that proved difficult considering the Great Depression happened during his term in office. Additionally, he lacked charisma and the ability to work well with other politicians and that, combined with his opposition to Prohibition, dominated the public's perception of his first term in office and worked to prevent his reelection.

He felt the main aim of a president was to avoid a dictatorship or Socialism and help all Americans through lawful regulations and humanitarian volunteerism. He practiced what he preached even prior to becoming president when he headed the Food Administration during World War II. A primary undertaking during that time was a program he implemented that banned certain foods on certain days in order to cut consumption of provisions needed overseas and to prevent rationing at home. For his efforts, the New York Times named him one of the ten most important living Americans.

Hoover had just begun to implement his prosperity expansion program of relief to farmers, protective tariffs, and expanded manufacturing when the stock market crash of 1929 occurred. In an effort to alleviate the sinking economy, Hoover extracted pledges from big business to expand construction projects, maintain wages, cut federal spending, doubled expenditures for dams, highways, and other public works in order to keep employment active. A serious drought in 1930, however, sank any hope of economic recovery and the resulting downward spiral caused unemployment to skyrocket and banks to fail.

The first unemployment assistance law, the Emergency Relief and Construction Act, was signed in the hope of providing relief. Hoover also deported 1.2-million Mexicans living in American barrios to relieve unemployment even though 60% of them were American citizens.

He expanded civil service coverage, set aside land for national parks and forests, doubled the number of Veteran's hospitals, constructed the San Francisco Bay Bridge, originated the Federal Bureau of Prisons, reorganized the Bureau of Indian Affairs, started construction of Boulder Dam (later renamed Hoover Dam), and waged war on the Mafia.

To pay for his government programs, the president passed the Revenue Act of 1932, which hugely raised income tax. Combined with increased national debt, millions on government relief, raised tariffs, and blocking trade, Hoover became the biggest tax and spend president ever to that date.

The crash that sent a booming economy into deep depression dominated most of his tenure and as the nation's leader during this dark period of American history, the public blamed him for the Depression even though it was not his fault. His reelection campaign was filled with hostile crowds and even a failed assassination attempt and he lost his reelection bid.

FRANKLIN DELANO ROOSEVELT

1882 - 1945

Thirty-second President of the United States

Presidential term: 1933-1945. Democratic Party. Roosevelt was a corporate lawyer and the only president to be elected to an unprecedented four terms in office. Citizens feared not having a regulated number of terms for a president could result in a monarchy or dictatorship so the 22nd Amendment, which limited a president's tenure to two terms, was eventually passed as a result of FDR's long occupancy.

In his early presidency there was such animosity between FDR and Herbert Hoover that petty actions on the part of the president against Hoover marred his proper demeanor. Roosevelt formed his "New Deal" policies in an effort to recover from the devastating effects of the Great Depression. He intended to give relief to the unemployed, help the economy recover, and reform banking and the economic system. Credit for many of those policies actually belonged to Herbert Hoover but Roosevelt simply changed their names and took sole credit for them. Hoover complained that his phone was tapped and his mail was opened but no investigation ever ensued. Roosevelt's pettiness even went so far as to strike Hoover's name from the immense dam being built on the Nevada/Arizona border and instead, called it Boulder Dam. The name would not be changed to Hoover Dam until years later. At first reclusive, Hoover eventually warned of a dictatorship trend with New Deal policies and became the voice of those who felt 'politically homeless' as a result of Roosevelt's New Deal. A liberal, Roosevelt's policies remained such until he tried to pack the Supreme Court in 1937 and conservatives ended New Deal expansion.

Federal agencies expanded during Roosevelt's tenure and unethical requirements for federal employment were employed, which worked to the benefit of the president. As an unspoken condition of employment, job seekers were expected to register and vote Democrat and contribute to Roosevelt's campaigns.

Struck by polio in 1921, FDR was permanently paralyzed from the waist down, a fact he tried very hard to hide from the public. He helped found the March of Dimes to assist those afflicted with disabilities.

In 1934, to make it easier to maneuver due to his infirmity, the Oval Office was moved to the southeast corner of the West Wing overlooking the Rose Garden where it remains today.

Two scandals haunted FDR's time in office. Warren Delano, Jr., his maternal grandfather, became rich off the opium trade in China and FDR was eventually discovered to have had a longstanding affair with Lucy Mercer, his wife's social secretary.

A major milestone in FDR's presidency was the passage of the Social Security system. It is one of the longest and most popular government programs in U.S. history and came about as a result of the Great Depression when senior citizen poverty exceeded 50%. The Act provided benefits to retirees and unemployment benefits were included in the original package signed by FDR in 1935. The program was financed by a payroll tax on worker's wages with half being paid by the employer and half from the tax on the employee's salary. In 1937 the U.S. Supreme Court case "Helvering v. Davis"[13] examined the constitutionality of social security when Boston resident George Davis sued regarding the legality of the tax but the U.S. District Court in Massachusetts upheld the tax. That decision was reversed by the Circuit Court of Appeals and then an IRS commissioner took the case to the U.S. Supreme Court which again upheld the validity of the tax. Payroll taxes were first collected and benefits first paid in the same year, 1937. Over the years, changes have been made to the original terms and the tax rate has increased several times. Disability benefits were added in 1956 and LBJ's administration added Medicare. A cost of living increase began in 1975 and during

President Carter's term he even went so far as to illegally grant disability benefits to immigrants who had never paid into the system. In the 1960s funds from individual social security trusts were placed into the General Fund as additional revenue for Congress. That irresponsible decision created a severe deficit crisis in the program that Americans face today.

FDR was the first president to make substantial use of radio in order to reach the public directly. He instituted a series of 'fireside chats' in which he pitched his policies. A main goal as president was to restore confidence in government with a series of programs. High unemployment plagued FDR throughout his administration but he continued Herbert Hoover's unemployment relief program after renaming it and went on to develop the Civilian Conservation Corps, or the CCC, which put a quarter-million men back to work in rural projects, established the National Labor Relations Board, formed the Securities and Exchange Commission to regulate Wall Street and named notoriously corrupt Joseph P. Kennedy to head it. The Tennessee Valley Authority (TVA) was created to stimulate the economy and Prohibition was repealed which brought in new tax revenues. He came under fire, however, when he assaulted Veteran's benefits and the issue was defeated by the Veteran's of Foreign Wars. FDR went on to reduce military salaries and naval budgets as well as reduce spending for education and research, which were not well received by the public.

When it became apparent during World War II that Hitler was exterminating the Jews, a delegation of Jewish leaders attempted to meet with President Roosevelt to urge him to bomb German railroad tracks so the Nazis would be unable to transport Jews to concentration death camps but Roosevelt claimed such action would divert resources from the war effort and refused to meet with them and took no action to obstruct Hitler's genocide. Tragically, had he met with this delegation and heeded their message, millions of Jewish lives would have been saved.

During his second term, the Fair Labor Standards Act set a minimum wage and a draft was imposed when America entered

World War II. When the U.S. Supreme Court declared several of his programs and policies unconstitutional, FDR retaliated by appealing to Congress to allow him to appoint five new justices, thus "packing the court" and making it possible for the president to control the court and continue his questionable policies. The unethical plan was soundly defeated.

Nevertheless, an unusual amount of deaths and retirements on the Supreme Court gave FDR the opportunity to appoint eight liberal justices anyway.

The powerful AFL and CIO split and weakened union support for the president during his last two reelections but FDR was a crafty politician and he manipulated delegates to the presidential convention and got the nomination for a third term.

Roosevelt instituted White House 'passes' in 1939 as well as closing the gates to the public upon the visit of England's king and queen. From that time forward the public no longer had free access to the 'People's House.'

After his success in maneuvering a third term, which he won by convincing voters that only he had the experience needed to lead the nation through difficult times, he continued to expand the Army and Navy and provided aid to U.S. Allies. FDR declared war on Japan after the surprise attack on Pearl Harbor on December 7, 1941 but the defeat of Nazi Germany had been FDR's real priority after Germany and Italy declared war on the U.S. Ultimately, however, Congress and the American people demanded FDR devote more effort against Japan.

In an astounding act of deplorable indifference to human suffering, FDR signed Executive Order 9066 that provided for the internment of 110,000 Japanese-Americans after the attack on Pearl Harbor. 62% were American citizens, which made his actions unlawful and unconstitutional but FDR carried it even further by seizing their property as well and ruining their lives despite the fact they were citizens who had done nothing wrong. In 1976 President Gerald Ford proclaimed FDR's actions as "wrong" and President Ronald Reagan signed the Civil Liberties Act of 1988, which was co-sponsored by Rep. Norman

Mineta (D-Ca) who was interred in a Wyoming camp. The Act provided a formal apology to Japanese-Americans as well as granting a $20,000 redress payment to surviving detainees. President George H.W. Bush appropriated additional funds in 1992 to ensure all remaining internees received their payments and offered another formal apology. By 1999, the final payment was made to 82,210 former detainees or their heirs at a cost of $1.6 billion dollars.

FDR was just as detached with the racial unrest in America. It was Eleanor Roosevelt who spoke on behalf of civil rights for blacks and did her best to influence FDR to promote a civil rights agenda and an anti-lynching law. FDR did nothing, however. He spent a great deal of time at a home he established at a therapeutic hot springs area in Georgia but Eleanor didn't spend time there because she didn't want to see the horrendous treatment of blacks in the area. Only after FDR began driving around the area with his secretary did he begin to realize the extent of racism but he still did nothing to alleviate it. Eleanor was the voice of conscience on the issue and never stopped her efforts on behalf of racial equality while FDR simply appeared to lack human empathy for others.

FDR came from a very privileged background where he was spoiled by his mother and made to feel he was entitled because he was a member of elite society.

Even his struggle with polio failed to instill compassion for others and although he was able to put on an affable public face, he was actually quite indifferent in private.

During his third term, the East Wing was built to accommodate the White House Military Office as well as the First Lady's offices. Eleanor Roosevelt became one of the most active and controversial First Ladies in history. Extremely liberal, she always championed causes of the underdog. Due to the president's longtime affair with Lucy Mercer, the First Lady was emotionally estranged from her husband and spent the rest of her life immersed in numerous social, political, and human rights causes.

Respected for his leadership skills and ability to produce results, FDR easily won a fourth term by persuading the nation that it would be dangerous to change leaders during wartime. His health, however, was quickly declining and he died of a massive cerebral hemorrhage on March 30, 1945.

His strong, if often controversial leadership carried the nation through the dark times of the Great Depression and WWII and ensured FDR's legacy as an extraordinarily effective president despite his appalling lack of concern or action on behalf of human rights.

HARRY S. TRUMAN

1884 - 1972

Thirty-third President of the United States

Presidential term: 1945-1953. Democratic Party. Truman was a small business owner and farmer. His simple down-to-earth common sense upbringing in America's Heartland formed his no-nonsense pragmatic approach to life. Due to FDR's rapidly declining health the Democratic Party recognized that their choice for vice president in the upcoming election would more than likely become president so they worked out a deal to rid the party of the unacceptable incumbent vice president and replace him with Harry Truman who was only vice president for 83 days when FDR died.

Perceived by the public as a "small time little man," Truman nevertheless had a reputation for hard work, honesty, and fiscal expertise and events that unfolded during his tenure soon changed the public's mind about his ability as a decisive leader.

A major foreign policy success for Truman was the Berlin Airlift. Ground access to the blockaded city of Berlin was denied so Truman ordered something that had never been tried before, sending mass numbers of military aircraft to drop food and supplies to those trapped in the city. This went on for months until ground access was again granted. A man of decision, Truman felt the only way to end the war and save millions of American lives was to drop an atomic bomb on Hiroshima and Nagasaki, which ultimately was responsible for ending World War II.

The post-war economy was unstable and inflation was extremely high. Debilitating labor strikes broke out including the railroad, which brought travel to a standstill. Truman vetoed curtailing power of the labor unions but his veto was overturned and the Taft-Hartley Act was placed into law to rein in the unions. Revolted at the shabby treatment of black soldiers, Truman signed Executive Order #9981 to desegregate the armed forces. His series of social programs were called the 'Fair Deal' proposals and were an extension of FDR's New Deal but they proved to be unpopular and the only one to be enacted was the Housing Act of 1949, which reshaped American cities with urban renewal programs.

An advocate of a pro-Israel state, Truman assisted in establishing the State of Israel. After World War II, Truman made huge cutbacks on defense because he felt using the atom bomb caused other nations to shy away from hostile action with the U.S. so defense spending could be cut. He changed his mind, however, with the outbreak of the Korean War.

Truman's approval rating was only 36% as he faced reelection and most people felt certain he would lose the election. The president decided to go directly to the people by criss-crossing the country by train, making 'whistle stops' and drawing huge crowds. The media ignored Truman's campaign while focusing on Dewey's race. They were so certain Dewey would win that the Chicago Tribune published an edition in error declaring Dewey the winner when in fact Truman had won.

During Truman's second administration, NATO was established to rein in Soviet expansion in Europe and a Communist witch hunt was launched against the government and citizens of the United States. FBI Director J. Edgar Hoover, along with Senator Joseph McCarthy, contended the government was riddled with Communists. Thousands of innocent people were fired as security risks causing many to commit suicide before the hysteria was found to be groundless.

In 1951, the 22nd Amendment was ratified which prevented presidents from running for a third term. Even though Truman was 'grandfathered' in and could have run again, his approval rating had plummeted to 22% - an all time low for presidents - as a result of the Korean armistice negotiations reaching a stalemate. Additionally, while Truman was working to prevent further escalation of the war, the Republican House Leader leaked information to the press regarding Truman's firing of popular General McArthur for promoting his own plan to attack China's supply bases. Truman was criticized for his dismissal of McArthur along with mismanagement of America's involvement in the Korean War but time proved his common sense, ability to reach strong and independent solutions, and his unfaltering leadership established him as one of America's great presidents.

(DAVID) DWIGHT EISENHOWER

1890 - 1969

Thirty-fourth President of the United States

Presidential term: 1953-1961. Republican Party. Eisenhower was a career soldier who gained immense popularity as the Supreme Commander of the Allied Forces in Europe. The ensuing D-Day invasion contributed to the eventual German surrender and was one of the most massive military operations to date. Eisenhower was so successful as it's leader that he became a legend.

In 1950, he went on to serve as the first Supreme Commander of the newly established North Atlantic Treaty Organization (NATO). His spectacular military career, strong leadership, and great popularity made him a natural choice for president.

Because of his war experiences, Eisenhower's term as president was spent on cultivating peace. He campaigned on the promise of going to Korea to end the war and he did just that six months after taking office when he was successful in obtaining a much sought after truce.

During his first term he expanded social security, reduced the military and introduced atomic weapons to relieve the need for large ground troops. He encouraged global cooperation in sharing atomic energy knowledge with an eye toward peace.

In 1953, Eisenhower changed the name of the presidential retreat from "Shangri-La" to "Camp David" in honor of his grandson.

One of his most monumental accomplishments which affects the nation even today was the 1956 Federal Highway Act, a coast-to-coast road system that would allow Americans to travel throughout the country via a modern interstate highway structure and bring auto travel into the modern day. It was a feat that changed and expanded the lives of all Americans.

Eisenhower easily won a second term and found it to be a busy one. Race relations were heated and the president was forced to send troops to Little Rock, Arkansas to enforce integration of the high school in that city. He was reluctant to support civil rights policies but nevertheless he signed the Civil Rights Acts of 1957 and 1960 into law. One objective of the laws established the Civil Rights Commission whose purpose was to enforce penalties against those who violated the voting rights of any U.S. citizen.

The Cold War between the U.S. and the Soviet Union was in full swing and the president was forced to deal with the U-2 incident in which a U.S. spy plane was shot down over Russia and led to strained relations between the two countries.

Further anxiety was brought about by Russia's 1957 launch of Sputnik, the world's first space satellite. That event placed the United States as subordinate in the space race so Eisenhower had to take aggressive steps to prove America's equal ability. The successful 1958 launch of the first American satellite restored the United States' international reputation and formulated NASA, the U.S. space program.

Both Alaska and Hawaii were admitted to the union in 1959.

Eisenhower's biggest failure as chief executive was in doing nothing to rein in the hysteria surrounding the 'Communist' witch hunt perpetrated by the notorious Senator Joseph McCarthy who was lax in his desire for facts or proof of Communist membership and whose committee resulted in unnecessarily ruining many, many lives.

The final confrontation of Eisenhower's presidency came in 1961 when the U.S. broke off diplomatic relations with Cuba after Fidel Castro seized American property in Cuba and charged the U.S. with counter-revolutionary exploits. Because the tense situation occurred at the end of Eisenhower's term, the outcome remained unresolved when he left office.

As a result of the Former Presidents Act, Eisenhower was entitled to a Secret Service detail, a lifetime pension, and a state provided staff after he left office.

Eisenhower's laid-back demeanor, congenial personality, ability to radiate hope and optimism for the future, and strong leadership guaranteed his legacy as a popular president, although one that was reluctant to hold the office. History ranks him as the last successful president with a character record that is above reproach.

JOHN FITZGERALD KENNEDY

1917 - 1963

Thirty-fifth President of the United States

Presidential term: 1961-1963. Democratic Party. Kennedy was a career politician and the only president thus far to win a Pulitzer Prize, a national literary achievement award for his book, *Profiles in Courage.* The first televised presidential debates were between JFK and Richard Nixon during the 1960 campaign, which Kennedy won in one of the closest elections in history to that date.

The Kennedy patriarch was Joseph Kennedy, well known as a ruthless and ambitious man who was determined that one of his son's would be the first Catholic president. JFK was raised in an extremely forceful and competitive family environment, yet his personality was so likeable that he was able to overcome the cutthroat perception of his father and achieve the presidency. His administration was known for its upbeat optimistic atmosphere and his youth and enthusiasm gave the country hope for the future that had been lacking.

Illness and a legendary sexual appetite never interfered with Kennedy's ability to lead and the elegance of Jackie Kennedy and the charisma and sophistication of the president generated a romanticized view of Kennedy's administration. It has been said they were the closest America has come to royalty and the designation of "Camelot" to describe the lifestyle of the Kennedy White House only perpetrated that belief.

Kennedy's 'New Frontier' progressive legislation included increasing the space program, senior medical care, federal aid to education, and civil rights programs.

During Eisenhower's administration a plan was conceived to overthrow Fidel Castro's regime in Cuba and JFK ordered it to proceed. 1500 Cuban exiles whom the U.S. had trained invaded the island but Kennedy failed to provide air support resulting in the capture of the exiles and the plan failed miserably. It not only was a major embarrassment to Kennedy's presidency, it also convinced Castro that the U.S. would invade again and led to the Cuban Missile Crisis.

When U.S. spy planes revealed Soviet missile sites in Cuba, JFK ordered a naval quarantine in which U.S. Navy ships inspected all vessels arriving in Cuba to prevent weapon shipments from being delivered. He further demanded that the missile bases be dismantled. After some macho posturing, Russia backed down and Kennedy quietly met with Soviet Premier Nikita Khrushchev. A treaty to end atmospheric testing of nuclear weapons was signed and the threat of disaster was avoided but the world would soon learn just how close it came to that possibility.

Kennedy worked to end the Vietnam War and signed National Security Action Memo #263 on October 11, 1963 to withdraw 1,000 troops but he was assassinated and his successor Lyndon Baines Johnson reversed the order escalating the war instead.

Foreign policy saw the president visit West Berlin In June 1963 to protest against the Berlin Wall in a speech where he said, *"Freedom has many difficulties and democracy is not perfect, but we have never had to put a wall up to keep our people in."* He formed the Peace Corps for Americans to volunteer in underdeveloped countries to help improve their lives.

He was strong in domestic policy as well, especially in civil rights issues. He intervened with 3,000 troops and federal marshals when James Meredith was denied admission to the University of Mississippi because he was black. He also assigned federal marshals to protect Freedom Riders and again intervened when Alabama Governor George Wallace blocked the door at the University of Alabama to keep two black students from entering. The Alabama National Guard and federal marshals changed Wallace's mind.

His assassination in Dallas on November 22, 1963 prevented President John F. Kennedy from having the time he needed to accomplish much but it also catapulted him to martyrdom and his place in history as one of the most beloved and admired presidents.

LYNDON BAINES JOHNSON

1908 - 1973

Thirty-sixth President of the United States

Presidential term: 1963-1969. Democratic Party. Johnson was a career politician who was born and raised in the poor hill country of Texas, LBJ retained a life long affinity for the average person and a desire to help make their lives better. Civil rights remained a primary focus of his presidency.

He was a complex man with many conflicting sides to his personality. He was a brilliant politician but fought personal demons that not only made life difficult for him personally but professionally as well. He had remarkable manipulative skills that eventually led to his reputation as the most powerful, effective, and influential Senate leader in history but his lust for power drove him to do unscrupulous things. His forceful and dominating personality twisted many powerful arms and his power of persuasion was legendary. His mood swings were extreme and he has been described by Dr. Bertram Brown, psychiatrist to many White House aides, as a megalomaniac. [14] Doris Kearns Goodwin was a long time aide and personal friend of Johnsons who describes him in her book as bi-polar/manic depressive.[15] At times his ego was so out-of-control that in one instance he even presented a bust of himself to the Pope and in the final years of his presidency he found it difficult to distinguish between fact and fiction or even between his own expectations and actual reality. At times his thoughts became so obsessive that he believed he was the target of some delusional conspiracy and his paranoia would cause him to lash out against others in irrational accusations. He felt he was entitled to whatever he wanted and did whatever it took to make it happen without a conscience. His thought process in the final years of his presidency became more and more psychologically problematic and throughout his life and presidency he remained much more a man of cunning than a man of character.

His 1948 Senate race against well-loved former Texas Governor Coke Stevenson was rampant with allegations of ballot stuffing[16] and Johnson not only won unfairly, he unnecessarily trashed the good name of a beloved public figure in the process. His 'win at any cost' approach to life made him a complicated and often disliked figure. Nevertheless, he went on to become the most feared but powerful and effective man in the Senate.

Johnson shrewdly combined his political and private expertise to form his basis for making millions. When Austin radio station KTBC went bankrupt in 1943, LBJ purchased it for only the debt owed and put it in Lady Bird's name to avoid any appearance of personal 'conflict of interest.' Broadcasting is dependent on the federal FCC for approval for its existence and expansion and as a federal senator Johnson sat on the Senate Commerce Committee which oversees the FCC. The success and subsequent expansion of KTBC was subtle but it made Johnson a millionaire and eventually led to his vast investments in land and banking.

In October 1964, shortly after Johnson became president, one of his long-time top aides, Walter Jenkins, was caught and arrested by Washington, D.C. police for making a sexual pass at another man in the YMCA bathroom. The scandal caused Johnson to order the FBI to do background checks on White House aides, something that had not been done prior to the Jenkins' incident.

As president, among LBJ's more crude and bizarre control techniques aimed directly at those of "culture" whom he disdained, was to hold meetings or even dictation while he sat on the toilet or compelled bureaucrats to swim naked with him in the White House pool.[17] He had a habit of humiliating people as a means of maintaining power over them.

During his term, Johnson initiated Medicare and Medicaid and was an advocate for civil rights. The Civil Rights Bill of 1964 virtually outlawed most forms of racial segregation and was followed by the Voting Rights Act that ended discrimination in voting. Additionally, LBJ appointed the first black Supreme Court Justice and went after the Ku Klux Klan.

The 1965 Watts Riot began a wave of violent riots across the nation that only worsened with the assassination of Martin Luther King in 1968. Johnson was fixated on not appearing to be weak in the eyes of the world so he ignored public opinion and President Kennedy's path toward peace and escalated the Vietnam War, thereby enraging American citizens.

The Gulf of Tonkin[18] incident was one of his final downfalls because members of Johnson's administration knowingly lied about the incident. Two American destroyers involved in a CIA classified program of covert secret missions to collect intelligence information on North Vietnam were allegedly attacked. The Pentagon, however, lied about one ship being attacked by the North Vietnamese in international waters. Two days later another clandestine operation occurred and the ship reported they were attacked as well and began firing back. Later data revealed that no attack actually occurred but the president was only presented with information that supported claims North Vietnam had attacked U.S. destroyers so he ordered planes to hit North Vietnam torpedo boat bases and fuel facilities. Congress passed the Gulf of Tonkin Resolution, which granted Johnson the exclusive authority to order military force without consulting the Senate and gave LBJ the justification he needed to greatly escalate the war. At the beginning of LBJ's presidency there were 16,000 troops in Vietnam. Seven years later there were 550,000 with a thousand soldiers dying a month. The nation was fed up but Johnson stubbornly refused to listen to experts and the American public in their demands to end the war. Protestors outside the White House chanted, *"Hey, hey LBJ, how many kids did you kill today?"* on a daily basis. LBJ later admitted he could hear the chants, which only served to intensify his weakening mental state.

Johnson was unyielding in his view that the Vietnam War had to be escalated because America simply couldn't be seen by the rest of the world as weak or losing. His constant messages of optimism and approaching peace spun a distorted tale to Americans that the Viet Cong couldn't match American military strength and the VC were on the verge of collapse. Then came the Tet offensive.

Previously, the might of the VC forces was obscured by their quick skirmishes in the jungle but the major extent of the Tet offensive brought enemy forces out in the open where they captured cities and exhibited their substantial strength, something not seen before by the American public. Johnson was forced to abandon his world of make believe and deal with the reality that the media and American citizens suddenly realized he had purposely kept the true nature of the war from them. Exasperation and loss of confidence in the president's handling of the war caused support for LBJ to drop to its lowest level. When he first began his presidency in 1963, a Gallup Poll indicated eight out of ten Americans approved of the way Johnson was doing his job. After the Tet offensive his approval rating dropped to a low 26%.

The media began running negative editorials and as Americans started realizing how badly Johnson had handled the war their level of trust in his ability to deal effectively with both domestic and international problems plummeted. By 1968, the majority of people felt LBJ had lied to them so they no longer trusted him in any sphere. He had lost his credibility.

To make matters worse, the presidential primaries were looming and the common denominator in the months before the primaries was the public expression of anger and frustration at the Johnson administration and the public's desire for change.

Despite the fact LBJ was an incumbent, the public took the avenue available to them to express their dissatisfaction by supporting Senator Eugene McCarthy and Bobby Kennedy instead of the incumbent president. A national state of unrest and discontent and the huge public backlash aimed at the occupant of the White House pulled Johnson back into the harsh glare of reality and made him realize he couldn't win reelection so, on March 31, 1968, he shocked the nation by announcing he wouldn't run for another term.

History will record Lyndon Baines Johnson as a master politician but one with a troubled personality. He actually accomplished much of note during his tenure but his ruthless nature and failure to realistically deal with the Vietnam War spawned a legacy mixed with both positive and negative.

RICHARD MILHOUS NIXON

1913 - 1994

Thirty-seventh President of the United States

Presidential term: 1969-1974. Republican Party. Nixon was a lawyer and the only person to resign as President of the United States.

Nixon was a secretive and reclusive personality who was often petty in his dealings with others. Described as sullen, sour, uptight, a loner, unpleasant, vindictive, square, paranoid, narcissistic, ruthless and humorless, his personality was a hindrance at times.

A favorite campaign tactic was to insinuate his opponent was supported by the Communist Party. It worked to get him elected to the House of Representatives and a membership on the Un-American Activities Committee where he forcefully prosecuted the Alger Hess spy case, thereby making a name for himself.

His presidential administration was referred to as an 'Imperialistic Presidency' because he retained a high level of control over government policies and decisions, traits that sometimes led to decisions he regretted. Eventually his downfall over decisions made regarding 'Watergate' would plummet the nation into collective trauma.

During Nixon's first year in office Astronaut Neil Armstrong became the first American to walk on the moon.

The unpopular Vietnam War was escalated under Lyndon Johnson's administration so Nixon began his tenure under taxing circumstances. Public outrage created turmoil and revolt and when four student demonstrators were killed at Kent State University, Nixon fought back at opposition to the war by instituting illegal wire taps, harassment, break-ins, and whatever means were at his disposal for exacting revenge.

In 1971 the *New York Times* published the secret 'Pentagon Papers' that revealed government intentionally misrepresented the Vietnam War to the American public. That revelation tremendously increased opposition to the war and led to the Nixon Doctrine in which American troops were replaced with Vietnamese troops. By 1973 U.S. troops had been withdrawn. The president was credited with orchestrating 'peace with honor' but returning soldiers were met with hostility and the nation continued to be in turmoil despite the end of the military conflict.

Nixon excelled in foreign policy and traveled to China where he was successful in opening diplomatic relations as well as establishing détente with the Soviet Union.

Domestically Nixon added an annual cost of living raise to social security, created Supplemental Security Income (SSI) to assist disabled and special circumstance recipients, enacted wage and price controls, implemented cuts in government spending, created the Environmental Protection Agency (EPA), Occupational Safety and Health Administration (OSHA), Drug Enforcement Agency (DEA), federal affirmative action programs, expanded school integration, developed a new anti-ballistic missile system, pushed through anti-crime legislation, and approved the development of NASA's space shuttle program. He was also the first president to visit all fifty states while in office.

In 1974, Vice President Spiro Agnew admitted charges of corruption relating to Watergate and resigned. He was replaced by U.S. House of Representatives Minority Leader Gerald Ford. Members of Nixon's Cabinet and advisors faced criminal charges and prison. Ultimately, the illegal and secret activities surrounding the burglary of the Democratic Party headquarters located in the Watergate Building, known as the Watergate scandal and leading directly to the White House, led to the resignation of Richard Nixon in the face of imminent impeachment...the only president to date to resign.

Even though Richard Nixon accomplished a great deal during his term as Chief Executive, the stain of Watergate and the dishonor it brought to the executive office resulting in his resignation will forever be the main occurrence for which he will be remembered.

GERALD FORD

1913 - 2006

Thirty-eighth President of the United States

Presidential term: 1974-1977. Republican Party. Ford was a lawyer and the only president to not be elected to either the vice presidency or the presidency.

He was born Leslie Lynch King, Jr. but after his mother divorced his father and remarried his name was changed to that of his stepfather.

President Nixon's Vice President Spiro Agnew resigned because of criminal charges so Ford was nominated and approved by Congress on December 6, 1973 to take his place, becoming the first person to be appointed Vice President under the 25th Amendment. He was Vice President for only eight months, as he became President when Nixon faced imminent impeachment and resigned over the Watergate scandal on August 9, 1974.

An avid Boy Scout as a child, Ford was especially proud of the fact he attained the highest level of scouting by becoming an Eagle Scout, the only president to do so.

The main function of his administration was to restore confidence in the Executive Office. His genial down-to-earth personality was just what the nation needed after Nixon.

Ford took office during a recession that was complicated by high unemployment and rising inflation, making his job more problematic. During his tenure he established a special education program for handicapped children, supported the Equal Rights Amendment, and shied away from moral matters, leaving the abortion issue to the states.

The Swine Flu pandemic swept the nation during Ford's tenure and caused public health officials to urge all Americans to become vaccinated but more people died from the vaccine than from the flu.

A U.S. cargo ship, the Mayaguez, was seized by Cambodia and Ford gained respect from the American people for his decision to use military action to free it. The last U.S. troops left Vietnam in 1975 as Saigon fell to the Communists.

Within the scope of his foreign policy Ford launched détente with the Soviets, which eased the Cold War.

Ford granted Nixon a full pardon for his involvement in Watergate because he felt the nation was in agony and it was time to end the suffering and move forward to bring honor back to the presidency. The public, however, was furious with Ford's pardon and it was clear that was the primary reason he lost his 1976 election bid. In hindsight, historians feel he made the right decision nevertheless.

In a 2004 interview with Bob Woodward of the Washington Post which was released after Ford's death as agreed to by Woodward, Ford stated he felt George W. Bush was *"wrong to lie to the public about weapons of mass destruction to involve the U.S. in an illegal war and had he (Ford) been president, he would not have gone to war."*

There were two unsuccessful assassination attempts on Ford, both by women, but at the end of the day the reluctant president proved to be a man of integrity and honor and he succeeded in bringing confidence back to the Office of President.

JAMES EARL "JIMMY" CARTER

1924 -

Thirty-ninth President of the United States

Presidential term: 1977-1981. Democratic Party. Carter was a peanut farmer and politician who was distantly related to both Elvis Presley and June Carter Cash. He was the first president to be born in a hospital and the only president to be interviewed by Playboy magazine.

Carter's meteoric rise from obscurity to the presidency was accomplished with the backing of powerful New World Order (NWO) associates and Carter's popular post-Watergate promise of providing open and honest government. The nation was still reeling from Watergate so Carter's appeal as a political 'outsider,' along with his devotion to his religious faith, helped him narrowly win the election over President Ford. His Secret Service name was "Deacon," which fit his image.

Known as a micromanager, Carter's presidency had to deal with a stagnant economy, double-digit inflation, high unemployment, severe fuel shortages, invasion of the American Embassy in Tehran, and the capture of American hostages. A frugal person, Carter cut the White House staff by one-third and ordered his Cabinet to drive their own vehicles.

Carter signed an executive order giving a full pardon to Vietnam War resisters, created a Cabinet level energy post, increased the social security payroll tax, removed government controls on commercial aviation, partially deregulated the rail, truck, oil, finance, and communication industries, and endeavored to reorganize the government.

A dedicated liberal, Carter focused on a global view of foreign policy and was a New World Order advocate. His presidential campaign was largely financed by the Rockefellers who felt Carter would further their Trilateral Commission goals for the purpose of creating a global economy power that was superior to political governments, thus creating a New World

Order. As president, Carter appointed numerous Trilateralists to key policy making positions. He returned the Panama Canal to Panama, initiated full diplomatic relations with China, and made human rights in foreign policy a mainstay of his presidency.

Carter worked toward peace efforts during his tenure and even more so after he left office. The 1978 Camp David Accords, a peace agreement between Israel and Egypt that was negotiated by Carter and took thirteen long days to achieve, was one of his most important accomplishments while in office.

The U.S. began secretly providing aid to anti-Soviet Islamic factions and when the U.S.S.R. invaded Afghanistan, Carter announced he would not allow any other outside power to control the Persian Gulf. He stopped the export of wheat from the U.S. to the U.S.S.R., which commenced tremendous hardship for American farmers. He also prohibited American participation in the 1980 Summer Olympics in Moscow. The Afghan policy of both President Carter and President Reagan helped create problems with Islamic fundamentalism that continue today.

During a six-month period in 1980, 125,000 Cuban exiles defected from Cuba in boats landing in southern Florida. Cuba's economy was so depressed that five men hijacked a bus and rammed it into the Peruvian Embassy to seek asylum, amid a hail of gunfire. An embassy guard was killed in the exchange of gunfire so Castro removed the remaining guards at which time 10,000 additional people crammed into the Peruvian Embassy for asylum. Because of the dangerous situation, Castro announced the Port of Mariel would be open to anyone wishing to leave. Castro packed the boats with criminals from the prison system and the mentally ill. The wave of boats arriving from Cuba overwhelmed the U.S. Coast Guard who was charged with detaining them and the immigration agencies that had to process them. Riots broke out in the detainee centers and President Carter was heavily criticized for his handling of the situation, especially in granting amnesty to undeserving and undesirable people.

The Shah of Iran was a long time ally of the U.S. yet Carter did nothing to help him when his administration was overthrown and refused him asylum in the U.S. Carter finally gave him a temporary stay in America so he could obtain cancer treatment. Allowing him into the U.S. so infuriated Iranian militants that they abducted 52 Americans hostages. [19] Attempts to rescue them failed but eventually negotiations were successful but Carter's biggest disappointment was that Iran intentionally punished Carter by refusing to release the hostages as long as he was president and they deliberately waited until a half-hour after Ronald Reagan was sworn in to release them, denying Carter the final satisfaction of seeing them released on his watch.

During his tenure, Carter was regarded as having shortcomings in his character as well as surrounding himself with less than honorable people. When his administration was over the GSA was stunned to find rotting garbage in the White House, furniture that had been ruined in the Eisenhower Executive Office Building, and other damage left by Carter's staff which caused GSA Manager Buddy Respass to declare that he had seldom met more "mean spirited people."

Largely considered a 'do-nothing' president, Carter tried to create a renewed confidence in government but his approval rating continued to drop. After leaving office Carter became very involved in global peace efforts and was awarded the 2002 Nobel Peace Prize for his efforts in helping to find peaceful solutions to international conflicts, advancement of democracy, and human rights. Inappropriately for a former president, he also became a vocal critic of George W. Bush's policies and administration as well as of other social issues for which a former president should remain neutral.

RONALD REAGAN

1911 - 2004

Fortieth President of the United States

Presidential term: 1981-1989. Republican Party. Reagan was an actor and the only president to be divorced or to have been in charge of a labor union (SAG).

His presidency began in dramatic fashion when the 52 American hostages that had been held for over a year by Iran were released only 30-minutes after Reagan was sworn in as president.

During his administration Reagan policies greatly harmed the economy of the nation and the middle class but in the aftermath of Vietnam, Watergate, and the Iran hostage situation, Reagan's charismatic personality, love of people, and genuine desire to do the right thing returned dignity to the Office of the President and restored pride in being American, a feeling that was sorely needed after the Carter administration.

Reagan's conservative Midwest upbringing never left him and throughout his life he remained humble, down-to-earth, and wholesome. A patriotic American, he got caught up in the hysteria of the McCarthy Communist witch-hunt during the 1950s while president of the Screen Actors Guild and was marred by rumors that he reported many Hollywood personalities to the FBI as Communists, which led to them being 'blacklisted' from the industry and totally ruined their careers and lives.

During his first term as president Reagan appointed Sandra Day O'Connor the first female Associate Supreme Court Justice. The federal debt escalated, unemployment was high, income tax rates were lowered but the payroll tax rate was increased, tax was imposed on social security and unemployment benefits, and he fired over 11,000 federal air traffic controllers when they refused to return to work in violation of the Taft-Hartley Act.

Despite fiscal decisions that favored the rich and made it more difficult for the middle class to further stretch their budgets, his endearing personality enabled him to win a landslide victory for reelection. Shortly after taking office for the second time the 25th Amendment was invoked for the first time as it pertained to a sitting president when Reagan briefly turned control of the government over to Vice President George H.W. Bush while he underwent a colon procedure for polyps.

Some of his policies brought public criticism, such as the president's refusal to deal with the HIV-AIDS crisis. He wouldn't even mention the name until actor Rock Hudson's death from AIDS forced the disease into the spotlight. Additionally, the president was staunchly against abortion, which angered women who felt the choice to abort or continue a pregnancy was a personal decision between themselves and their doctor and should not be a political issue.

Another low point was Reagan's handling of illegal immigration. The 1986 Immigration Reform and Control Act made it illegal to knowingly hire illegal immigrants and required employers to verify their status but the public criticized his bleeding heart approach to granting a one-time amnesty to 3-million illegals. Public opinion felt that action rewarded people who became criminals the minute they illegally sneaked into the U.S. and was unfair to those who came to America in a legal manner, learned the language, assimilated into the culture, and became productive citizens. George W. Bush later disregarded Reagan's promise of a one-time amnesty by following the same path as Reagan.

The biggest mistake of Reagan's presidency, however, was the Iran-Contra Affair.[20] Members of Reagan's executive branch sold guns to Iran who was an enemy of the U.S. and illegally used the profits to fund anti-Communist rebels in Nicaragua. Reagan claimed to not know anything about the scandal but told the public that the weapons were *not* part of a hostage exchange after the disgraceful event was revealed to him. The matter resulted in eleven convictions and mass criticism that the president should certainly be aware of what his security advisers were doing. History grades the Iran-Contra Affair as one of the top ten biggest mistakes made by U.S. presidents.

Reagan moved away from President Carter's foreign policy diplomacy and took a hard line escalating the Cold War. His style was criticized as 'warmongering' until the rise to power of Soviet Premier Mikhail Gorbachev who instituted new policies of reform and openness. At that point Reagan shifted to a diplomatic approach and commenced several summit meetings with the new Soviet president that resulted in the ban of U.S. and Soviet intermediate-range nuclear missiles from Europe and eventually brought about a peaceful end to the Cold War.

By the end of his administration the national debt had quadrupled, his economic policies were largely failures, and Reagan had proven to be only mediocre as a leader. While the public may have been disappointed in the president's leadership skills, they forgave him any failings and continued to love and be loyal to a man who symbolized all that was good in America.

His wife was largely seen as a difficult and demanding elitist who tried to impose an imperialistic tone to the Reagan White House but the president always kept the atmosphere ordinary and comfortable. Even in the face of controversy history rates Reagan as one of the most beloved presidents who was an eternal optimist with a wonderful sense of humor and a genuine love of people.

GEORGE HERBERT WALKER BUSH

1924 -

Forty-first President of the United States

Presidential term: 1989-1993. Republican Party. Bush was an oil executive and only the second sitting vice president since Martin Van Buren to be directly elected to the presidency.

An amazing and ironic coincidence concerned a shared date as presidents by George H.W. Bush and his son George W. Bush. Bush, Sr. officially declared the start of the first Gulf War with his address to Congress on 9-11-90. The attack on the World Trade Center that began the war with Afghanistan during Bush, Jr's presidency was 9-11-01.

Bush was a member of Yale's secret Skull and Bones Society, which is considered to be an elitist group working toward a New World Order in which the rich would be in control of the globe. He was unusually influenced by the NWO philosophy and even spoke about it in his inauguration address *after taking the Oath of Office to uphold the Constitution!* He again promoted the concept in his 1991 State of the Union address, which angered many Americans.

Foreign policy was a main focus of Bush's administration. After the U.S.S.R. was dissolved Bush and Mikhail Gorbachev declared a partnership that ended the Cold War.

Negotiations for NAFTA (North American Free Trade Agreement) began with Canada during Bush's tenure.

Panama's president, General Manuel Noriega was using the Panama Canal to facilitate the drug trade from South America to the U.S. and after Panamanian forces killed a U.S. officer in December 1989 Bush ordered a military invasion of Panama using 25,00 U.S. troops to depose Noriega.

The Persian Gulf War commenced with the August 1990 invasion of Kuwait by Iraq. Bush organized an immense international force and carried out a successful war in the region for which he gained the public's respect.

The tragic "Ruby Ridge"[21] debacle happened under Bush's watch in August 1992 resulting in the death of an innocent mother and child at the hands of federal agents who were never held accountable and suffered no consequences. [22]

Randy Weaver and his family lived in a remote mountain top cabin in the northern Idaho area known as Ruby Ridge. An undercover ATF informant befriended Weaver with the goal of infiltrating the Aryan Nations organization not far from Weaver's home. Weaver was not a member of the group and did not condone their activities but was willing to accommodate the informant's request for firearms as Weaver needed the money. The informant stated he wanted *"sawed-off shotguns, the shorter the better"* and supplied Weaver with the firearms and instructions on the length he wanted. He then bought the guns back from Weaver, which ensured Weaver had violated federal weapons laws. The informant then sawed the barrels shorter than legally allowed by law, which an Idaho jury later declared to be "entrapment."

After the informant was exposed the ATF tried to recruit Weaver to inform on the Aryan Nation in exchange for dismissing minor weapons charges. Weaver refused. The ATF filed charges and lied to a Grand Jury telling them Weaver was a suspected bank robber with criminal convictions. The Grand Jury handed down an indictment and fourteen months after the gun sale Weaver was arrested.

He was sent a summons for a court date but the date in the letter didn't match the date given Weaver so he failed to show up and a warrant was issued. A Grand Jury again indicted Weaver as a "fugitive." At that point Weaver rightfully felt the government was "out to get him" and isolated himself in his mountain cabin.

ATF began surveillance to determine the family's routine and installed hidden cameras around the property. On August 21, 1992 armed U.S. Marshals went up to the property to prepare for a military style assault but Weaver's dog detected them and began barking. Randy, his son Sam, and a family friend went to investigate. When the dog detected someone in the bushes, Marshals shot it and Sam fired in the direction of the marshals not knowing who the intruders were. The marshals returned fire killing the 14 year old *as he ran away*. The family friend shot and killed a marshal and the next day the FBI took over and ordered "deadly force" which was later declared to be "unconstitutional" by a Justice Department task force. Nevertheless, an FBI sniper shot and killed Vicki Weaver while she stood behind a door with her infant in her arms. An armored personnel carrier was brought in despite the fact no shots were fired from the Weaver cabin. A ten-day standoff ensued and Weaver finally surrendered.

At his trial Weaver was acquitted of all charges except missing his original court date and of bail condition violations and spent four months in prison. Twelve FBI agents were disciplined for covering up their illegal actions and for trying to destroy all copies of the FBI's internal report on Ruby Ridge. Nothing happened to the sniper. The case against him was dismissed and he was later promoted. The President was a former CIA director so Bush received massive public criticism for allowing agencies under his watch to perpetrate such an inexcusable horror. Public faith in federal law enforcement plummeted during this dark period in American history, never to be the same again.

The lingering economic recession of the late 1980s and continued high unemployment combined with the president's unwillingness to remedy the situation, contributed to Bush's defeat for a second term in the White House. The public viewed him as 'out-of-touch' with the common man. During his first campaign for the presidency Bush dramatically said, *"Read my lips; no new taxes"* and then went on to inflict them, which caused most Americans to no longer believe him. His approval rating dropped to a low 29% during his tenure but despite the fact many Americans viewed him as being out-of-touch and were appalled by his endorsement of the New World Order philosophy and upset that he went back on his promise to not impose new taxes, he left office with a vastly improved 56% rating.

WILLIAM JEFFERSON "BILL" CLINTON

1946 -

Forty-second President of the United States

Presidential term: 1993-2001. Democratic Party. Clinton was a lawyer who knew at a young age that he wanted to be in public service. Two events brought about his decision to seek public office; a meeting with President John F. Kennedy as a youngster and listening to Martin Luther King's "*I Have a Dream*" speech. He is a Rhodes Scholar who met his wife Hillary Rodham at Yale. After graduation he became involved in politics and served as Governor of Arkansas before running for president.

Clinton grew up in an alcoholic household and a region that valued 'macho' over moral integrity. Hot Springs, Arkansas had been known for decades as a hotbed of backroom criminal enterprises that included protection rackets, vice, gambling, prostitution, and graft. Money and power reigned and influenced local attitudes and home life. In a culture where women garnered little or no respect, it was acceptable for men to drink, abuse their wives and girlfriends, and have affairs on the side. Cities like Las Vegas and Hot Springs drew excitement seeking personalities like a moth to a flame so Clinton's 'party girl' mother and biological 'playboy' father fit right in. It's not surprising then that genetics, environment, and influence of the indulgent 1960s resulted in the contradictory nature of Bill Clinton. Those factors, combined with growing up in an alcoholic household, helped form the complex personality of the 42nd president.

A Rhodes scholar who was able to read by age three, and a governor who was ranked the fifth most effective governor in the nation in 1986 and the best national governor in 1991, Clinton had the ability to be an above average president but his ethical and moral behavior was consistently at odds with those efforts.

Despite his imperfections, Clinton was a cheerful, charismatic, and well-liked president who sincerely cared about others. As the nation's leader, however, he failed to keep his promises, compromised his principles, and it soon became apparent his word could not be trusted. Honesty was not a priority for him and he was not straightforward with others. He was unpredictable and changeable and had a habit of blaming others for his problems. His difficulty in making decisions made him appear wishy-washy and indecisive, he was constantly late, unorganized, and his lack-of-control caused him to act before thinking, leaving him with regrets on more than a few occasions.

According to Ronald Kessler in his book, *A Matter of Character*, both Clintons were "chameleons" who could charm people publicly but were nasty and temperamental and rudely ignored the staff that served them in private. Kessler cites the example of a White House usher who was the father of four and had taught Barbara Bush how to use her laptop. After she left the White House she encountered problems with her computer and called Mr. Emery, who assisted her. When Hillary found out, she fired him. For a year he was unable to find a job but the Clintons never lost a minute's sleep over causing hardship for his family. Kessler maintains a selfish and nasty character will manifest itself in a president's judgment and job performance and history seems to agree.

Throughout his tenure as president Clinton consistently took a strong stand on various issues only to back off when criticized so he earned a reputation as a 'compromiser.' He was limited in what he could accomplish because he was saddled with a Republican Congress who subjected him to constant personal attacks and great animosity due to the fact the Republicans were very conservative and greatly disliked Clinton's compromising situations with women outside of his marriage.

Hillary Clinton took a strong role in government affairs that the public viewed as inappropriate and the president was criticized for allowing such a situation. In addition, both Clintons were under scrutiny for their involvement in the "Whitewater Affair," a series of questionable real estate and bank deals that occurred when Clinton was governor of Arkansas. No formal charges resulted but it did tarnish his presidency.

In February 1993 the first bombing of the World Trade Center made America aware of terror on its own soil. An Islamic terror cell parked a rented van filled with 1500 pounds of explosives in a basement parking garage and the resulting explosion killed six people and injured 1,000 in the World Trade Center building. The mastermind was caught and imprisoned but because of the event, Clinton was made aware of future terrorist activities aimed at the United States but remained lax about prevention.

Another sinister time in American history involving federal agents occurred with the horrific February 1993 Waco Branch Dividian compound massacre[23] of dozens of innocent people at the hands of U.S. federal agents.

The Branch Dividians were a religious sect headed by David Koresh. They had broken away from the Seventh Day Adventists Church and eventually settled in a large site east of Waco, Texas called Mount Carmel.

The ATF claimed the compound contained a number of illegal firearms so agents intended to serve a search warrant on February 28, 1993. Rather than knock on the door and serve the warrant, a military assault approach was used instead. Federal agents caused the religious group to believe they were under attack and the end of the world was happening. It later became apparent an encounter was unnecessary because months prior to the raid Koresh invited ATF agents to come to Mount Carmel and talk but they refused.

The resulting confrontation began a 51-day siege in which the complex was burned to the ground and 76 people were killed.

Louis Freeh was appointed FBI director in 1993 but he had no management experience and punished anyone who disagreed with him. His heavy handed style contributed to a variety of problems at headquarters and in the field, with

Waco becoming a monumental embarrassment. His aversion to computers and his directives to those who worked for him to not use them, resulted in information chaos but Clinton failed to remove him despite disastrous consequences for the bureau. Freeh remained until George W. Bush's administration.

Heading the tactical team was FBI Agent Rich Rogers, the same agent that was heavily criticized for his actions at Ruby Ridge prior to the Waco debacle. His actions in interfering with negotiation teams at Waco would again land him in trouble. Increasingly aggressive tactics were employed against the compound and armored tanks were even used to destroy buildings and vehicles. High volume noise and music was inflicted 24-hours a day and power and water were cut off.

Government agents didn't understand the Dividians' religious zeal and felt they were going to commit suicide so the agents increased their assault by punching holes in the building and pumping in tear gas. Fire engulfed the building and everyone inside died. Despite overwhelming evidence of government negligence and illegal behavior, only the surviving Dividians who left before the final assault, were prosecuted. As happened in Ruby Ridge, no action was taken against federal agents and the event served to further alienate the public from federal law enforcement, heighten disrespect for government officials who took no disciplinary action, and diminish respect for the president.

Timothy McVeigh was so horrified by the Waco siege that he drove from Arizona to Waco to find out for himself what was happening and was photographed by the FBI. In retaliation for Ruby Ridge and the Waco siege, McVeigh blew up the federal building in Oklahoma City[24] in April 1995 – two years to the day that the siege at Waco ended in tragedy.

Although Clinton's tenure was marked by grim events, his presidency enjoyed a stable prosperous economy, low unemployment, a balanced budget, and a federal surplus for the first time since 1969 due in no small measure to the proliferation of the new computer age and the dot com industry. Crime was down and the U.S. was not involved in any war. During his first term the Family & Medical Leave Act was passed which required employers to allow employees unpaid leave for medical or family emergencies. NAFTA was ratified and the Brady Bill was passed, which made a five-day waiting period mandatory for the purchase of a handgun. Low income workers were assisted by expansion of the Earned Income Tax Credit and Hillary attempted a universal health care reform plan, which died due to intense public as well as American Medical Association and health insurance industry pressure. Toward the end of his first term Clinton appointed Madeleine Albright as the first female U.S. Secretary of State. Tax cuts for low income families and small businesses along with implementing spending restraints, rounded out Clinton's first term.

His second term was dominated by the Monica Lewinsky sex scandal for which Congress impeached Clinton for lying to a grand jury. The proceedings dragged out but didn't contain much zeal and Clinton remained in office to complete his term, leaving with a healthy approval rating. In the end, more time and taxpayer money was spent on going after a president because he lied about a sexual encounter than has been spent flushing out corruption or making a future president accountable for lying to the nation about his intent to wage war.

Clinton signed the Gramm-Leach-Bliley Act 1999, which repealed the Glass Steagall Act of 1933 and hugely contributed to the subprime mortgage financial crisis of 2007-2008 and the resulting deterioration of the nation's economy. The Glass Steagall Act of 1933 established the FDIC (Federal Deposit Insurance Corporation) whose purpose was to reform financial institutions and control speculation. Immense conflicts of interest saddled people with big tax increases as a result of the repeal because it allowed commercial lenders to underwrite and trade mortgage backed securities and collateralized debt obligations to the detriment of the national economy.

Operation Desert Fox was launched to weaken Saddam Hussein's power over Iraq and Operation Allied Force was a bombing mission against Yugoslavia to stop ethnic cleansing and genocide.

An interesting side note of a personal nature during the Clinton administration revolved around their daughter Chelsea. In his book, *Inside the White House*, Ronald Kessler relates occasions the White House staff, and especially the White House usher and chefs, had with numerous "first children." Without exception, they cited previous presidential offspring as pampered, spoiled, and difficult – except Chelsea. Even though the presidency is exceptionally demanding on the time of both parents, the Clintons nevertheless were totally devoted to their daughter. They always made sure she received all the time and attention she needed while, at the same time, instilling a sense of responsibility toward others that prevented her from feeling she was more entitled than other people. They carefully guided her into an adulthood that was grounded, which allowed her to grow into a remarkable young woman.

On page 221, Kessler quotes his interview with Assistant White House Chef Sean Haddon who said, *"Chelsea is widely respected by the White House staff as an unspoiled teenager. She is a wonderful kid who tries very much not to be a problem and whatever we want to give her (food) is OK with her."* Regardless of how the nation may perceive her parents, the Clintons were good parents who managed to raise an exceptional daughter.

Clinton's charisma and love of people made him an exemplary ambassador to any nation he visited or any foreign head that came to the White House. The U.S. was the recipient of many friendships forged with global leaders as a result of Clinton's diplomacy.

The national deficit was in the red when Clinton took office but by the time he left it was in the black. The economy rebounded under his watch and more foreign leaders than at any time in history were on friendly terms with the U.S. due directly to Clinton's unique talent for winning friends. Some in society had reservations about whether the moral lapses in his character and the witch hunt that resulted from it interfered with the ability to do his job but the President left office with a vigorous 68% approval rating and his accomplishments speak for themselves.

GEORGE WALKER BUSH

1946 -

Forty-third President of the United States

Presidential term: 2001 - 2009. Republican Party. Bush was an oil businessman and politician whose complex personality contributed to his legacy as one of the most controversial presidents in the history of the U.S.

He is the son of a former president, which has occurred only once before when John Quincy Adams became president after his father John Adams previously served in that capacity.

Bush's mother was a Pierce before her marriage to George Herbert Walker Bush and was not only the daughter of McCall magazine's publisher, but also traced her lineage back to the 14th president Franklin Pierce.

Bush won the presidential election in a bitterly contested race whose outcome was eventually decided by the U.S. Supreme Court. Seldom has a race been so close and decided by the electoral college vote rather than the majority popular vote.

Each state's respective parties choose individuals from a formula that depends on the number of national representatives and senators from the state to make up the electoral college. If a particular candidate wins a state's popular vote by even one vote, with very few exceptions *all* the state's electoral college votes go to that candidate. Simply put, majority popular vote does not decide elections – electoral college votes do.

Such was the case with the acrimoniously disputed election of 2000, which hinged on the outcome of Florida's ballot fiasco. For five weeks lawyers for both the Bush and Gore campaigns battled it out in the courts, even taking the problem to the U.S. Supreme Court, which eventually ruled it was too late for a recount and awarded Florida's electoral college votes to Bush. To the country's credit, once the bitter battle was over the nation accepted George W. Bush as their leader and put the election issue behind them.

While George Herbert Walker Bush held his staid east coast lifestyle with his elitist friends and Yale cronies in high regard, his son spent the major part of his life in Texas where life was down-to-earth and unpretentious. In Texas, a handshake and a person's word are their honor so Bush simply said what he meant, confronted issues head on, and didn't waltz around topics to avoid dealing with subjects. He was a 'tell-it-like-it-is' person who never lost the common touch. Those roots made him different from his father and east coast ivy league establishment but the fact still remained that Bush was born with a 'silver spoon' in his mouth and enjoyed a privileged upbringing that left voters wondering if he possessed enough 'merit' to overcome his fortunate advantages. It also made him fodder for a mean spirited media who made a sport out of presenting the president as a backwards cartoon character due to his casual dress and tangled speech. Presenting him through an unflattering lens rather than presenting a fair and honest account of events often resulted in slanted coverage.

Bush followed in his father's footsteps and was educated at Andover, Yale and Harvard but held a lifelong disdain for those who were snobbish, felt they were intellectually superior, pompous, elite, and full of themselves. He was never affected by the uptight ivy league atmosphere and instead, displayed his typical 'rebel' spirit by refusing to wear a coat and tie to class and sitting in the back in his bomber jacket spitting chew into a cup. As co-owner of the Texas Rangers baseball team he spurned the air-conditioned luxury of the owner's sky box to sit on the bench behind the dugout in his inexpensive suit and boots with the Texas flag etched on them. He preferred to be an every day person and his rebel spirit remained with him as president to enable him to run his administration with a grounded and confident manner, secure in who he was. He was not a materialistic person or someone who worried about appearance or other people's opinion of him. As long as he felt he was doing the right thing and made the right decision he never looked back or second-guessed himself. Bush felt strong leadership would well serve the president's oath, which is the most minimal of any in government and consists only of a commitment to preserve, protect, and defend the Constitution. He intended to do it with bold and decisive action appropriate to the circumstance regardless of how popular or unpopular that action might be viewed by others.

The media ridiculed Bush for his infamous smirk and swagger but Bush good naturedly dismissed it by responding, *"Some folks look at me and see a certain swagger, which in Texas is called 'walking.'"* Those that knew him best said that because he was the president, he was often unable to be publicly candid about what he really thought or felt so his smirk was a telltale mannerism that revealed his dislike for the person, situation, or statement that had just occurred. Due to his unaffected nature he was especially likely to do this when in the presence of what he felt was pretense or a charade.

His run-ins with the English language, or 'Bushisms,' were legendary and the president was good-natured about his verbal jumblings and the first to poke fun at himself. He didn't take himself too seriously. He was compared to former president Harry Truman in that Bush was fixated on not sugarcoating his words. He valued straight talk and definitive action but listened to his advisors, asked intelligent inquisitive questions that got to the core of an issue, read all the data on a subject, weighed the pros and cons, made up his mind, put an issue into motion and never second guessed his decisions once they were made.

Karl Rove, a former aide to Bush's father, was nicknamed 'Bush's Brain' and managed his presidential campaign. Bush's past included DUI citations, allegations that his father's influence obtained draft evasion service for his son, and a party lifestyle that could have been a public relations problem for Rove but in the summer of 1986 while visiting his parents in Kennebunkport, Maine, Bush became a 'born again' Christian and turned his life around after talking with family friend the Reverend Billy Graham. He viewed life though a moral lens so his frequent references to religion enlisted the support of the powerful ultra-conservative Christian Right, which helped him win the presidency.

When the Bush administration moved into their offices, they found the 'w' key removed from computers, obscene voice mail messages, and desk contents all over the floor, among other disrespectful things left by the Clinton administration. In all, the GSA audit showed $15,000 of deliberate damage. Bush was determined to return dignity and respect to the offices for which taxpayer dollars paid and made it clear to his staff that no such nonsense would happen under his watch.

Unlike some former administrations that demonstrated total disregard for their staff, both George and Laura Bush were always considerate of others and did thoughtful things such as making sure their Secret Service agents had a plate of food when they were at events and thanking their staff for little things they did for them. He sincerely liked people and their ideas and was a good listener who had a well developed sense of humor that made him engaging to those he met and with whom he worked. Also unlike some former occupants of the White House, the intoxicating and rarified atmosphere of the Office of President never twisted Bush's value system. He remained firmly rooted and continued to be the same down-to-earth person he always was.

Too often new administrations were not prepared to begin work the day after the inauguration but the Bush transition was organized and he was ready because his father had impressed upon him the importance of having his staff and organizational structure in place right down to the secretaries by the time he took office. To this end his father recommended Dick Cheney to assist in Bush's choices. Cheney ill-advised Bush to surround himself with Cheney's cronies, among them, John Ashcroft and Donald Rumsfeld who were driven by self-serving hidden agendas that were in conflict with what was best for the country. Over time the damage done by those closest to the president became apparent and they were replaced but at a huge disservice to the president and at great cost to the American public.

Bush thought 'outside the box' and believed in using existing programs if possible to enact policies rather than create new bureaucracies. There were many organizations that assist the needy, for instance, that didn't get federal funds and Bush felt allowing them to compete for those funds would tremendously cut down on starting from scratch in developing yet another organization for the same purpose.

Secrecy was his biggest downfall and most contributed to the nation's feeling that government was not transparent. It caused the American people to distrust a government and administration that they perceived as not forthcoming and hiding information from the people it was supposed to represent and protect. While at Yale, Bush was inducted into the secretive Skull and Bones organization where he learned to keep things close to the chest and where many of his lifelong close friendships were formed. That may have been a contributing factor regarding his proclivity for secrecy.

Only months after taking office the tragic events of September 11, 2001 occurred plunging the nation into a different way of life forever. Vowing to find and bring Osama bin Laden to justice, Bush's approval rating skyrocketed to 90% and he invaded Afghanistan in October 2001. When bin Laden escaped capture Bush simply changed the reason for being in Afghanistan, claiming the U.S. needed to "bring democracy" to the nation instead.

Debunking claims that Bush planned to invade Iraq even before he took office, the CIA revealed it actually began to take shape a little less than a year before the invasion. Bush didn't need a link between Iraq and the events of 9/11 because he already had grounds to go after Iraq if he wanted because Iraq had been violating U.N. mandates to disarm since the first Gulf War. Additionally, Bush gave Saddam Hussein the option to disclose the country's weapons programs or leave Iraq to avoid war rather than simply invade. In the end, however, false claims of Iraqi weapons of mass destruction (WMD) became the rationale for the March 2003 invasion making Bush the first president in history to order an unprovoked pre-emptive attack and military occupation of a sovereign nation against the will of the U.N. and the American people. When it was discovered there were no WMDs, there was a huge backlash of criticism regarding the handling of both the Afghanistan and Iraqi Wars and Bush became the first sitting president to cause the United States to be removed from the U.N. Human Rights Commission. Calling himself a "war president," the court of public opinion's approval rating dropped drastically to 24%, the lowest level of any president in 35 years. Nevertheless, Bush admitted his darkest days were the ones when he had to meet the grieving families of troops he sent to war or visit the soldiers who came home severely wounded. *"I do a lot of crying in this job,"* he once observed.

An old trick often used by government to gain support and blur the public's knowledge about the actual intent of a bill that is not in the public's best interest is to give it a name that belies its actual intent. Such was the case with the Patriot Act, which was passed within an astounding 43 days of the World Trade Center attack and has been viewed with great suspicion in the years since 9/11. Under the guise of a 'national security measure' to better fight terrorists, it has since been discovered that many bills prior to 9/11 that circumvented civil liberties had been included in the Patriot Act and were rammed through Congress before proper review and public debate could discover them. The bill may have been given an emotionally charged name for the time in order to enlist public support but it has been discovered to contain many sections that are directed more at the average citizen than suspected terrorists and time has proven that these laws can and have been abused. This huge and complex volume of new laws was presented to Congress in such a short time following 9/11 that many find that suspicious and mind boggling considering how slow government moves. Public opinion has made it clear that terrorism can be fought without giving up a free and open society but Bush claimed so many powers never before commandeered by a sitting president that the nation no longer resembled the blueprint set down by the Founding Fathers.

Even members of Congress began questioning the legality of the Patriot Act and a few even introduced legislation to curtail it. Then-Attorney General John Ashcroft toured the country giving speeches before law enforcement supporter-only audiences in an effort to authenticate the bill. Eventually cities, counties, and even entire states passed resolutions condemning the Patriot Act and refused to assist the Feds in their enforcement. It remains a grave threat to a free society because the majority of actions resulting from it can and are used against innocent citizens rather than just on suspected terrorists.

The Bush administration set a record for the largest annual deficit to date in U.S. history, in large part due to the cost of invading and occupying two countries at a price tag of over $10-billion a month. He also spent the U.S. surplus, which effectively bankrupted the U.S. Treasury. During the final months of his administration the nation experienced an unprecedented crisis of home foreclosures and bank institution failures. It's not surprising then that the nation faced a seriously declining economy and recession.

Bush forcefully pushed for Social Security reform but the public distrusted him and his proposals were unsound. Congress resisted his efforts and the issue was shelved.

Fall-out over his dismal failure to help New Orleans after Hurricane Katrina further caused his approval rating to sink. His incompetent leadership left the city in shambles and victims remained homeless years after the tragedy while Bush focused on expanding his war instead.

One of the more disturbing bills signed into law by Bush was the "Military Commissions Act of 2006."[25] It permitted the government to prosecute unlawful enemy combatants by military commission rather than by a regular court, *eliminated* habeas corpus, and allowed the president to determine what constitutes torture. While detaining prisoners at Guantanamo Bay without the right to legal counsel became an issue, it was conveyed that under the Geneva Convention only lawful combatants who conducted their operations in accordance with the laws of war were entitled to rights but those who deliberately attacked civilians outside the perimeters of the Geneva protection, were not. Regardless, it also had the chilling possibility of being used against every day citizens as well.

Habeas corpus was not the only long standing liberty protecting law to fall victim to the president's pen. Posse Comitatus soon followed. A federal law was passed in June 1878 as a result of the post-Reconstruction era of the Civil War, which limited the power of the federal government to use the military for state and local law enforcement reasons. The Posse Comitatus Act remained intact until October 2006 when HR5122, the "John Warner Defense Authorization Act" eliminated this long standing law in the face of national unrest due to the lingering Afghanistan and Iraqi Wars. Public objection to the elimination of Posse Comitatus soon reversed the Warner bill and in 2008, HR4986 was introduced to change the wording back to the original text. When signing the bill, a defiant president made sure he had the final word by attaching his own "signing statement" that made it clear the Executive Branch did not feel bound by the changes enacted by the repeal.

Illegal immigration became a delicate and very volatile issue all during the Bush administration and divided America in a way that hasn't been seen since the Lincoln presidency during the Civil War. Those who immigrated legally, went through the process to become Americans, learned the language, and desired to become part of the fabric of their adopted country, felt betrayed when Bush pushed programs to by-pass the citizenship procedure required of those who immigrated legally and gave them privileges denied to legal immigrants or even native born Americans. Despite the fact American citizens loudly and persistently objected to the special treatment of an illegal invasion, Bush intentionally and systematically ignored public opinion and did nothing.

Bush practiced 'double speak' when he expressed concern with containing the flow of illegal aliens while doing nothing to actually halt it. Abraham Lincoln did the same thing with the slavery issue. His strategy of paying lip service to freeing the slaves while actually doing little about it was a guideline for Bush's treatment of the illegal immigration situation. Romanticized history portrayed Lincoln as the "emancipator" of the slaves yet over and over he not only made it clear he didn't object to slavery, his true aim was to work toward a centralized government geared toward economic development and corporate subsidies. Had he sincerely been interested in ending slavery he would have followed the example of other countries like the British Empire who ended slavery peacefully through compensated emancipation but while he gave lip service to freeing the slaves, he turned a blind eye and did nothing so that slave owners would continue to have their cheap labor and he would be closer to his economic objective. In the same vein, Bush followed Lincoln's strategy with the Mexican illegal invasion.

While Corporate America reaped the benefits of cheap labor and recognized the president supported that wish, American citizens suffered. Illegals were first and foremost, criminals. The mere meaning of the word 'illegal' should have been enough to deny them entry but they arrived covertly by the millions with little or no consequence. A tremendous amount of work was outsourced so jobs were not plentiful to begin with but they went to illegals before Americans because illegals were willing to accept substandard salaries. Americans were willing to take jobs given to the illegals but the wage scale had been systematically suppressed to the point that a majority of jobs no longer paid a livable wage so Americans couldn't afford to live on what employers were paying because of the illegals. The economic impact on the social service system from the crush of illegals was devastating. Hospitals were required to care for them without fee while American born citizens went without care because they couldn't afford health insurance or out-of-pocket medical expenses. Illegals received welfare benefits denied to many deserving low-income Americans. Illegals enjoyed special low interest loans to start businesses those born in America couldn't get. Extra expense was required for language interpretation in schools and in printing government and voting documents. The largest drug trade came across the Mexican border bringing a huge criminal element with it. The expense of hiring more law enforcement to deal with the imported criminals, the cost of building more and more prisons, and the expense to the taxpayer to pay for the prosecution and incarceration of these criminals while they overcrowded the prison system, was only the tip of the iceberg when one considers the cost to the victims, which too often included loss of loved ones either through violence or drugs. Illegals stringently insisted on doing everything they could to avoid assimilating into the culture of America or even learning the language and the cost of Bush's tolerance toward the illegal invasion was simply staggering and devastating. The result was the same as in Lincoln's time; it divided America and left a nation in shambles.

Another controversy arose over the unprecedented dismissal of seven U.S. Attorneys in December 2006 by the U.S. Department of Justice. The scandal ignited a firestorm of controversy and criticism that resulted in a congressional investigation. The dismissed attorneys had all been appointed by President Bush and confirmed by the Senate over four years prior to dismissal. Allegations were that some of the targeted attorneys were fired to stop investigations of Republican politicians while others were fired for not investigating Democrats in an effort to damage their careers. No clear answers came of the investigation but defiant U.S. Attorney General Alberto Gonzales along with several other high-ranking Department of Justice officials resigned over the scandal.

Bush antagonized North Korea by calling them the "axis of evil" and relations between the two countries became strained. North Korea flexed their muscles by detonating a nuclear device in October 2006. Ultimately, North Korea agreed to dismantle their nuclear program by the end of 2007 upon the release of frozen funds in a foreign bank account.

On March 23, 2005 a trilateral agreement statement was reached at Baylor University in Waco, Texas between U.S. President George W. Bush, then-Prime Minister of Canada Paul Martin, and then-President of Mexico Vincente Fox called the

Security and Prosperity Partnership (SPP)[26] to implement a NAFTA super highway that many feared could lead to a borderless North American Union consisting of a combination of all three countries. The agreement statement was made without any public debate or Congressional authority, approval, oversight, or even review. It was simply imposed upon the American public.

As part of the SPP agreement, goods manufactured in China would arrive in sealed containers by ship to the Port of Lazaro Cardenas in Mexico to bypass the Panama Canal and be off-loaded to trucks that would take them to Larado, Texas where they would enter a super highway specially built for NAFTA purposes. Due to the secrecy surrounding these meetings and decisions, rumors circulated that the super highway was simply a precursor to a new borderless region called the North American Union and that U.S. Administrative Law was being rewritten into a new trilateral configuration to allow that occurrence. No proof to support that theory surfaced but Congress found it disturbing enough to propose Resolution 40 introduced by Rep. Virgil Goode in January 2007 identifying a North American Union as a "a threat to U.S. sovereignty." The American public was not consulted and the president was never held accountable for his secret activities regarding the SPP.

Not only did deceit and disinformation became a political hallmark of Bush's presidency,[27] resignations and scandals were also common in his administration including the Scooter Libby disgrace. President Bush dispatched then-Ambassador Joseph Wilson to Africa to 'discover' information that Iraq was purchasing uranium to make weapons of mass destruction. That alleged information would have justified Bush's invasion of Iraq but Wilson found nothing and refused to say otherwise. Retaliation came on July 14, 2003 when a public 'leak' was made that Wilson's wife, Valerie Plame, had been a covert CIA operative for over twenty years. The public disclosure put her life in danger and ended her career. Libby was fingered as the person that publicly disclosed her CIA connection and a congressional investigation ensued. Libby was convicted of obstruction of justice and perjury in helping to cover up the leak but it was later determined that columnist Robert Novak was the source most to blame for revealing Plame's identity. He called a CIA official prior to printing his piece to advise that he was going to refer to her in his column despite the fact there was no legitimate reason for him to do so. The CIA official told Novak that would cause problems for her and asked that Novak not name her but he did so anyway. After sorting through the facts, Bush commuted Libby's sentence, which resulted in severe criticism of Bush's abuse of presidential clemency power.

Personal and business connections between the Bush family and the Saudi Royal Family clouded the president's actions regarding the Iraqi War and a long laundry list of critical scrutiny included mishandling of both domestic and foreign policy, mismanaged war efforts, Abu Ghraib torture and prisoner abuse, justification for the invasion of Afghanistan as hunting down Osama bin Laden for the 9/11 tragedy and then declaring him 'no longer a focus' when he was allowed to escape due Bush's lack of leadership, lying again about bogus weapons of mass destruction in Iraq which he used to justify invading that country, elimination of habeas corpus (due process), unconstitutional presidential 'signing statements,' NSA warrantless surveillance of innocent American citizens, destruction of goodwill in nearly every nation, his bungled efforts following Hurricane Katrina, refusal to deal with illegal immigration, penchant for secrecy, and failure to be honest with the American people among others. As America began to realize the extent of Bush's destruction in trying to run the country, his approval rating plummeted drastically to a nearly all time low of 24%.[28] Eighteen out of twenty-one countries surveyed in 2006 felt Bush's administration was "negative for world security."

Bush wanted to confront problems and solve them, leaving the country in better order than he found it but history may show the 43rd president as one that accomplished little because his entire presidency and focus was consumed with a war effort. He was a president that was unwavering in his determination to do things his way regardless of what the American people or his advisors had to say. Having accomplished little of note during his terms, he nevertheless inflicted grave injury to America's free and open way of life[29] with his numerous attacks on liberties protected under the U.S. Constitution.

At the end of Bush's eight-years at the helm, the average American citizen was much worse off than they were before Bush's administration. Wall Street was struggling, the housing market was in the toilet, unemployment was at record breaking levels, families were unable to make ends meet and the nation was in a deep recession. The Afghanistan and Iraqi Wars bankrupted the deficit to the point it would take future generations to rebound from it and to many individual civil liberties had been curtailed. While it is too soon to evaluate Bush's legacy, history may ultimately give Bush a 'mixed bag' review as a president who had more than his share of failures but who did the best job he could. In the end, he will likely be remembered for his eternally upbeat optimistic personality, engaging manner, self-depreciating humor, down-to-earth nature, and decent character. His personality may ultimately fashion his legacy as much as his deeds as president.

BARACK HUSSEIN OBAMA II

1961 –

Forty-fourth President of the United States

Presidential term: 2009 – Present. Democratic Party. Obama was a community organizer, Illinois state legislator, and one-term U.S. Senator. The cloud of controversary that surrounds him makes him one of the least known personalities in the American presidency.

He was born on August 4, 1961 to Stanley Ann Dunham, a Kansas native and Barack Obama, Sr., a native of Kenya. His place of birth has never been resolved as the president refuses to produce his Certificate of Live Birth and had all his personal records sealed so the question of his legal elibibility for the presidency has not been answered. This has caused distrust throughout a major part of the nation's population.

Obama's parents divorced when he was two and his mother married an Indonesian man and moved with her son to Jakarta where he attended elementary school. In his autobiography, *Dreams From My Father*, he described the school as "a Muslim school" and admitted he studied the Quran. He returned to Hawaii where he lived with his maternal grandparents from fifth grade through high school. After graduating, he attended Occidental College in Los Angeles, Columbia University in New York City, and Harvard Law School. He did some law work in Chicago where he became a 'community organizer' and then a member of the Illinois legislature. The nation first took note of Barack Obama in July 2004 when he delivered the keynote address at the Democratic National Convention in Boston, an event that catapulted him to the U.S. Senate. Three short years later, he ran for President of the United States – and won. He is admired as an exceptional orator despite the fact he relies almost entirely on tele-prompters when he speaks publicly.

Voters knew very little about this former Illinois state legislator and U.S. Senator who didn't even complete his first term before running for president. Early in his campaign, disturbing evidence began to surface regarding his past associations with unsavory people as well as concern about his unorthodox political and social views. His own book, *Dreams From My Father*, produced references to his Socialist leanings and left half the nation hesitant about where he would take America if elected.

The liberal media drove the election of Obama almost to the exclusion of any coverage of his opponent and pushed him to power without prudent examination of who he really was and what his interpretation of "change" would mean to every American citizen. Their frenetic bias in favor of Obama prevented rational examination of legitimate concerns and charges by a more moderate and responsible media. That created an environment ripe for deceit and resulted in the election of a man who was surrounded by a cloud of unanswered questions, the most basic of which was on what soil he was born and in what direction he intended to take the nation. Nevertheless, on November 4, 2008 voters elected the nation's first African-American president. Only time and history will reveal his true character and intent for the United States.

Chapter 9

PRESIDENTIAL QUOTES

The following quotes from each president paint a written picture of the climate of their time and reveals how each administration remained true to the blueprint of the nation or affected the manner in which the Constitution was implemented or circumvented. The paths these forty-four men chose have brought us to the crisis we face today and make the fact evident that the nation was born in a struggle for freedom and has again reached a point of struggle to hang on to or regain those freedoms. We have come full circle.

"Whoever wishes to foresee the future must consult the past; for human events ever resemble those of preceding times."

~ Machiavelli; 1469-1527
Italian Political Philosopher

1) George Washington

"I walk on untrodden ground. There is scarcely any part of my conduct which may not hereafter be drawn into precedent."

This quote demonstrates Washington's mission as the first president of the United States. He was encumbered with developing the duties and blueprint of the first executive office knowing full well that future presidents would have to abide by the guidelines he set forth.

2) John Adams

"A Constitution once changed from freedom can never be restored. Liberty once lost, is lost forever."

President Adams was part of the original 'core' group of brave men who put their lives on the line to form a free society and enact a Bill of Rights and a Constitution that would be the guideline for the successful running of the new nation. Failure to follow strict adherence to the Constitution would gradually cause the nation to deteriorate with each succeeding president after the Founders.

3) Thomas Jefferson

"I have no fear that the result of our experiment will be that men may be trusted to govern themselves without a master."

This pure and optimistic vision from a main Founding Father held so much hope during this timeframe. Should future administrations fail to maintain states' rights, it would result in one federal 'master,' which was the fear expressed by Jefferson.

4) James Madison

"If tyranny and oppression come to this land, it will be in the guise of fighting a foreign enemy."

President Madison was perhaps the most insightful of all the Founders and his view of war was almost clairvoyant in regard to the future. The Revolutionary War, the Barbary Coast War of his predecessor, and the War of 1812 during his own administration caused him to reflect on the progressive destruction of rights granted under the Bill of Rights, which he authored. The excuse for impinging on individual freedoms was that it "was necessary in the best interest of the nation," a notion that greatly disturbed him.

5) James Monroe

"It is only when the people become ignorant and corrupt, when they degenerate into a populace, that they are incapable of exercising their sovereignty."

As America settled into the comfortable routine of freedom, citizens started to become complacent and their silence and emerging apathy frightened Monroe and caused him to fear for the hard fought self-governing of the new nation.

6) John Quincy Adams

"Posterity: You will never know how much it has cost my generation to preserve your freedom. I hope you will make good use of it."

It was important to President Adams that upcoming generations understand that freedom was not free and many of the Founders paid with their lives, the lives of loved ones, their property, even their own freedom so future generations could live in a free and open society.

7) Andrew Jackson

"I weep for the liberty of my country when I see at this early day of its successful experiment that corruption has been imputed to many members of the House of Representatives and the right of the people have been bartered for promises of office."

Jackson more than most presidents was cruel and coldhearted, especially in dealings with Native Americans. His abhorrent 'Indian removal' campaign resulted in the heartbreaking Trail of Tears tragedy and makes his profession of concern for his country ring hollow. He blamed others for his mistakes as his fingerpointing at Congress illustrates. Loss of integrity and credibility in the executive office was an unfortunate by-product as well during this dark time in history and began a migration away from the vision the Founders had for the Chief Executive.

8) Martin Van Buren

"It affords me sincere pleasure to be able to apprise you of the entire removal of the Cherokee Nation of Indians."

Marching farther down the road of presidential dishonor, Van Buren actually took pride in assisting Jackson in the dreadful and tragic Trail of Tears. The intent of the Founders was all but forgotten and America moved farther away from the Bill of Rights and the U.S. Constitution with this presidency.

9) William Henry Harrison

"The people are the best guardians of their own rights and it is the duty of their executive to abstain from interfering in or thwarting the sacred exercise of the lawmaking functions of their government."

President Harrison's intent was to return integrity to the office of the chief executive. Unfortunately for America, he died within weeks of taking the presidential oath.

10) John Tyler

"In 1840 I was called from my farm to undertake the administration of public affairs and I foresaw that I was called to a bed of thorns."

Tyler reluctantly filled Harrison's entire term, which was packed with turmoil as a result of inheriting the distress caused by both Jackson and Van Buren's terms in office. He followed the principles of the Founders and was a states' rights president, which caused him further conflict with an ever increasingly self-serving Congress.

11) James Polk

"There is more selfishness and less principle among members of Congress than I had any conception of before I became President of the United States."

As Presidents Tyler and Polk discovered, Congress proved to be government's biggest headache and blockade as corruption in the lawmaking branch became more and more prevalent. Implementing strict adherence to Constitutional guidelines became more and more difficult for presidents who did their best to follow in the footsteps of the Founders.

12) Zachary Taylor

"I have no private purpose to accomplish, no party objectives to build up, no enemies to punish ... nothing to serve but my country."

President Taylor's term was so short that his impact was negligible. He professed good intent but threatened to send an armed military into the South to prevent secession so violence was temporarily avoided by his death.

13) Millard Fillmore

"May God save the country, for it is evident that the people will not."

Emotions were becoming more heated between the North and South as a result of southern dissatisfaction with paying high tariffs for northern goods and the slavery issue became the justification for escalating tensions that were beginning to divide the nation. Clearly, President Fillmore felt fearful that the strain placed on the new democracy might cause fractures in its intent.

14) Franklin Pierce

"The revenue of the country, levied almost insensibly to the taxpayer, goes on from year to year increasing beyond either the interests or the prospective wants of the Government"

President Pierce was not a strong leader but he had a noble foresight regarding the greedy and unjust course Congress was taking in imposing unreasonable taxation on the people. He recognized that once Congress was successful in obtaining taxes that were morally wrong and felt the power that went along with requiring citizens to do their bidding, that it would not stop. While he felt sincere compassion for those required to unjustly meet those requirements, he also felt a sense of helplessness to prevent or change it as well.

15) James Buchanan

"The ballot box is the surest arbiter of disputes among free men."

Buchanan was ineffectual in resolving issues facing his administration. Faced with southern secession, he simply did nothing and failed to deal with the issue altogether. The above quote illustrates that he preferred for other avenues than himself to make decisions.

16) Abraham Lincoln

"Inasmuch as they (blacks and whites) cannot so live, while they do remain together there must be the position of superior and inferior and I, as much as any other man, am in favor of having the superior position assigned to the white race."

Lincoln made it clear over and over again that slavery was never his motive for starting the Civil War; secession was. A cunning strategist, Lincoln used the slavery matter simply as a political maneuver to distract the public from the real issue.

17) Andrew Johnson

"Outside of the Constitution we have no legal authority more than private citizens and within it we have only so much as that instrument gives us."

President Johnson was prevented by a Lincoln saturated Congress from upholding and advancing states' rights or from correcting the great lie perpetrated by Lincoln that the federal government formed the states and therefore, states' rights were a moot issue. Despite Johnson's best efforts, Congress gained more influence by enforcing Lincoln's centralized but erroneous view of government and the country began an adaptation of the Constitution that the Founders feared. America changed from a states' rights seat of power to a centralized federal seat of power, which not only violated the U.S. Constitution but forever changed the basic form of government.

18) Ulysses S. Grant

"The right of revolution is an inherent one."

Grant spent his entire career as a soldier and felt plunder was one of the 'spoils' of war. As a result, his post-war efforts in regard to Native Americans and the railroad were based on pure greed. His administration wreaked of scandal and the Republican Party became one of money and corruption, not freedom.

19) Rutherford B. Hayes

"It will be the duty of the Executive, with sufficient appropriations for the purpose, to prosecute unsparingly all who have been engaged in depriving citizens of the rights guaranteed to them by the Constitution."

The ballot box was especially crucial during the years immediately following Lincoln's administration and a political dance ensued between presidents who were determined to rewrite history by carrying on Lincoln's great deception and presidents that were untainted in their desire to follow the Constitution and the path set forth by the Founders.

20) James Garfield

"He who controls the money supply of a nation, controls the nation."

Garfield's observation would seem to be either a blueprint for bureaucrats or a warning to citizens to be vigilant. He was only president for four months, two of which he was barely cognizant, so his presidency had virtually no impact on history. It would appear, however, that his image for his administration was a capitalistic one that may or may not have moved farther away from issues of freedom.

21) Chester Authur

"The extravagant expenditure of public money is an evil not to be measured by the value of the money to the people who are taxed for it."

Authur was a confusing mixture of Republican greed and cronyism and concern for the quandary of the every day citizen. He was known for his integrity yet he did little to promote the public good during his four years in office. Government was neutral during his term, which allowed the nation to catch its breath.

22) Grover Cleveland

"Office holders are the agents of the people, not their masters."

A man of unquestionable integrity, Cleveland ran his administration on behalf of the people that elected him and felt the power belonged to the citizens of the United States and elected officials, including the president and Congress, were supposed to do the peoples' will, not the other way around.

23) Benjamin Harrison

"We Americans have no commission from God to police the world."

Harrison spent a great deal of his term on foreign policy and his extensive knowledge in that regard caused him to believe that the U.S. should not take sides in the business of other sovereign nations but should agree to let them conduct their business in the way they see fit.

24) Grover Cleveland

"I have tried so hard to do right."

Cleveland served two terms in office but Benjamin Harrison separated Cleveland's two terms with his own presidency. During Cleveland's second term he was encumbered with the large Republican spending of Harrison's administration and did all he could to bring the U.S. back to economic stability and advance agendas that were in the best interest of the American people.

25) William McKinley

"It's all a man can hope for during his lifetime...to set an example...and when he is dead, to be an inspiration for history."

McKinley may have hoped for a resplendent legacy but he fell far short of what he hoped to attain. He followed many of Lincoln's leads, which only created hardship for the American people and moved the nation closer to World War I. The Republican platform and McKinley's actions as president only served to create more turmoil as decisions moved further away from the intent of the Constitution.

26) Theodore Roosevelt

"To announce that there must be no criticism of the President is morally treasonable to the American public."

Teddy Roosevelt was perhaps one of the most intriguing and completely unaffected presidents in history. He was a 'man's man' that loved everything rugged and challenging but he was secure in who he was and the public knew that the persona Roosevelt presented to the public was genuine. His time in office was spent on his own terms, not those of the Republican party, and the nation was a bit better off for it.

27) William Howard Taft

"No tendency is quite so strong in human nature as the desire to lay down rules of conduct for other people."

Taft's heart was in the judiciary branch of government so he was happiest after he left the presidency and was appointed Chief Justice of the Supreme Court. He felt the court system was superior to other branches of government so his time as Chief Executive was neutral and further hampered by his inability to get along with others, which even included those within the Republican Party.

28) Woodrow Wilson

"The government, which was designed for the people has got into the hands of the bosses and their employers…the special interest. An invisible empire has been set up above the forms of democracy."

Wilson's presidency was marred by a failing economy and America's entry into World War I as well as his suppression of war protests and riots. In direct contrast to the intent of the Founders, he allowed himself to be unduly influenced by Socialist leaning advisors. The environment was ripe for special interest corruption and they took full advantage of it, to Wilson's dismay.

29) Warren Harding

"America's present need is not heroics, but healing; not nostrums, but normalcy; not revolution, but restoration."

World War I ended during Harding's term and he wanted to restore normalcy for the nation but his own administration was wracked with scandal. The executive office was overwhelming to him and his inability to be a strong leader gave Congress more room to maneuver in their best interest rather than the nations.

30) Calvin Coolidge

"To live under the American Constitution is the greatest political privilege that was ever accorded to the human race."

Coolidge was well equipped to restore confidence in the Office of President and did so during his administration. He believed in the vision of the Founders and did much during his six years in office for the middle class.

31) Herbert Hoover

"Prosperity cannot be restored by raids upon the public Treasury."

Hoover furthered the capitalistic goals of the Republican Party but the Great Depression occurred during his term, which gave him pause regarding his position on corporate greed.

32) Franklin D. Roosevelt

"The point in history at which we stand is full of promise and danger. The world will either move forward toward unity and widely shared prosperity - or it will move apart.

FDR's numerous agendas created a "political parent" situation where programs were in the hands of the centralized federal government rather than with the states. While the country needed guidelines to recover from the Great Depression and three previous Republican administrations, the long term affects of some of FDR's myriad programs served to take the country farther down the path of Socialism and some of his actions were actually found to be unconstitutional (internment of Japanese-American citizens), morally wrong, and clearly outside the intent the Founders had for the nation. FDR made great strides in pulling the nation out of chaos but in contrast to his above quote, the price Americans paid along the way was to actually become more divided as a result of some of his questionable policies.

33) Harry S. Truman

"When even one American who has done nothing wrong is forced by fear to shut his mind and close his mouth…then all Americans are in peril."

Truman agonized over the fact black soldiers put their lives on the line in service to their country but were still segregated and had to keep their anger to themselves. Truman changed that. The hysteria surrounding Sen. Joseph McCarthy's pursuit of Communists caused widespread intimidation. Innocent people were being accused and anyone was a possible target. Truman had the courage to make hard decisions and fought against those that dishonored the intent of the Founders.

34) Dwight D. Eisenhower

"The history of free men was never really written by chance but by choice; their choice!"

Ike clearly understood that the ballot box determined what path the country would follow for the term of the chosen president. As a soldier, Eisenhower was a good choice at this juncture to deal with the Cold War and the end of the Korean War but he was a disappointment regarding civil rights and his refusal to stop Sen. McCarthy's Communist witch-hunt. America chose a popular president but a largely ineffective one who placed the nation in 'neutral' for the duration of his term.

35) John F. Kennedy

"The very word 'secrecy' is repugnant in a free and open society; and we are as a people inherently and historically opposed to secret societies, secret oaths, and secret proceedings."

As government continued to move farther away from the intent of the Constitution and the federal government expanded, it also became more secret. The public was prevented from knowing about issues that affected their lives and futures and Kennedy was concerned about that.

36) Lyndon Baines Johnson

"A president's hardest task is not to do what is right, but to know what is right."

Doing the right thing was always a struggle for LBJ as his climb to success was at times, on the ladder of unscrupulous behavior. His entire political career was intertwined with the Brown brothers, who formed the private military corporation (PMC) of Brown and Root and became rich on no-bid government contracts compliments of their benefactor LBJ during the Vietnam War. While Johnson accomplished some important results for the nation, his sweetheart deals and even ballot stuffing were hallmarks of his career and that type of secrecy was harmful to the way of life the Founder's intended for America.

37) Richard Nixon

> *"A public man must never forget that he loses his usefulness when he, as an individual, rather than his policy, becomes the issue."*

The secrecy surrounding the Nixon administration is legendary and the criminal behavior of Nixon and his top aides in the Watergate scandal that brought down the presidency showed both the dark side of how far a president could go to trample the Constitution but also, that the people were still the final authority in demanding that their president possess the integrity necessary to lead the land in an honorable way - even if it meant impeaching him or demanding his resignation.

38) Gerald Ford

> *"In all my public and private acts as your president, I expect to follow my instincts of openness and candor with full confidence that honesty is always the best policy in the end."*

In direct contrast to Nixon, Ford was known to be a direct and trustworthy man. He did much to restore dignity and faith to the Office of President. The public became infuriated when he pardoned Nixon but even that act was done in good faith because Ford felt if he didn't do that, the nation's open sore would just continue and America wouldn't be able to put the issue to rest and move forward. In the end he was right and his three years in office began a time of healing.

39) Jimmy Carter

> *"Republicans are men of narrow vision who are afraid of the future."*

Carter may not have held Republicans in high regard but his own 'vision' was less than principled. His candor about working toward a globalized 'New World Order' contaminated the presidency as the intent of the NWO is in direct contrast to the Constitution's guidelines. Carter's rise to power was manipulated and financed by a group of capitalist elitists whose aim was a global economy that would protect them and give them world power. In that vein, Carter accomplished little during his term but tried to lead the nation down a path that would not have been in its best interest.

40) Ronald Reagan

"Man is not free unless government is limited."

Reagan recognized and often commented on the dilemma of ever expanding government, which he was unable to contain during his administration as well. His homespun manner and eternal optimisim made the public forget that he contributed to the devastating aftermath of Sen. McCarthy's 'Communist scare' by turning in entertainers he believed might be traitors, whether he could prove it or not. Americans also forgave him for botching events such as the Iran-Contra affair, the immigration issue, a huge national debt, and failing economic policies. As a president, Reagan was largely ineffective and made life more difficult for the middle class in an effort to protect his wealthy friends but as a person, he was well loved. His congenial personality made Americans feel safe and made him one of the most treasured presidents in history.

41) George H.W. Bush

"Read my lips ... no new taxes."

Bush came from privilege and was constantly accused of being out of touch with the every day person, which undoubtedly affected his decisions as president. He continued the Lincoln and Republican agenda on behalf of the wealthy and centralized government and the public lost trust in his promises after he raised taxes despite vowing otherwise.

42) William J. Clinton

> *"To realize the full possibility of this economy, we must reach beyond our own borders, to shape the revolution that is tearing down barriers and build new networks among nations and individuals, and economies and cultures: globalization. It's the central reality of our time."*

Clinton continued the New World Order agenda to benefit the upper echelon of society and let down the average citizen by signing the NAFTA agreement, which tremendously impacted on jobs and economic stability for the average American. The focus of modern day Chief Executives has continually moved away from freedom issues and taken the path of economics instead.

43) George W. Bush

> *"The true history of my administration will be written 50 years from now and you and I will not be around to see it."*

Regardless of everything said and written about George W. Bush, he remained his own man and his deep faith guided him to do what he truly felt was right. He made colossal blunders in judgment, some as a result of poor advisors and some from his own lack of knowledge and stubbornness. Loss of civil liberties was the big loser resulting from his administration, especially after 9/11 when government went into "over-kill" rather than reason. Freedoms were systematically eliminated under the guise it was "necessary" in order to fight terrorism. A free and open society continued to disappear under the guise of "national security" - just as James Madison predicted. The path George W. Bush chose to follow as the leader of the so-called 'free' world was a mixed bag of good and bad and the above quote is likely to be quite correct...history will define Bush's administration through the lens of time. It is too soon to determine his legacy but it will become clear in the years to come if history is reported in an honest manner and not rewritten as is so often done.

44. Barack Hussein Obama

"I found solace in nursing a pervasive sense of grievance and animosity against my mother's race."

America's newest president boasts that he intends to be a 'color blind' leader who will not focus on race, yet writings in his own books label the grandmother who raised him as *"a typical white woman."* His books set forth his preference for black culture and his affiliation for Muslims. He has stated, *"I will stand with the Muslims should the political winds shift in an ugly direction."* He has made public statements that ignite racial tension and help divide the races rather than unite them. When a president considers any criticism of his policies to be 'racist,' then the nation is in deep trouble. Obama's views were of concern when he was only a candidate. Where he stands on his allegiance to the United States, its citizens, the Constitution, and democracy will determine the direction of the country itself.

* * * * * * * * * *

"A Constitution once changed from freedom can never be restored. Liberty once lost, is lost forever."

~ John Adams, 2nd President of the United States

"A dictatorship would be a heck of a lot easier, just so long as I'm the dictator."

~ George W. Bush, 43rd President of the United States

These two statements demonstrate the extremes America has experienced...from the optimistic and pure vision of the Founding Fathers to a nightmare scenario where the liberties granted by the U.S. Constitution could be circumvented or eliminated. Bush made the above comment in jest but it showed an appalling lack of wisdom, responsibility, and common sense for a sitting president to utter such a statement even if he was just joking around. Such a thought would never have even entered John Adams mind as he and the other Founders put their lives on the line for the freedom that George W. Bush so cavalierly dismissed with his thoughtless comment. Significant freedoms and personal liberties have diminished one small step at a time over the centuries so a statement like Bush's instills fear in a nation that realizes it has come a long way from the 1700s and a situation described by Bush could actually happen under the right circumstances in the climate of the 21st Century.

The great experiment in democracy began with the American Revolution, which freed the colonies from the cruel oppression of England's harsh and restrictive rule. The Founders had such pure intent and total faith in the document they laid out to ensure the freedom of all American citizens. It was a document that could work over time if it was not corrupted.

Lincoln forever changed the origin of power by flip-flopping the intent of the Founders. By denying the southern states their Tenth Amendment right to secede, he slaughtered the basic form of states rights government set forth by the Constitution and created a centralized federal government instead. Government "by the people" was never the same after that 'great lie' was accomplished.

The presidency of George W. Bush brought America to its knees with a devastating loss of freedoms and individual liberties as a result of 9/11. His image of the nation as being easier to run if it were a dictatorship demonstrates the extent to which America has changed its attitude from a new land free to make its own choices that would benefit its residents to a nation that now depends on the government instead. The Founders deemed it necessary to enter the American Revolution to start a new and free way of life rather than continue being 'safe' but dependent and oppressed under England's rule. Lincoln created a similar situation by changing the seat of power from the states and making American citizens supposedly 'safe' but dependent on a centralized federal government, a condition that continues today. We have come full circle

"Whenever any form of government becomes destructive of these ends, it is the right of the people to alter or to abolish it....when a long train of abuses and usurpations [occur]...it is their right, it is their duty, to throw off such government ... "

~ U.S. Declaration of Independence

No experiment in democracy has ever lasted more than 200 years so it appears America's timeframe may be in peril. Paths of cho ice over the decades have led the country right back to where it began. It is mired down in corruption and bureaucracy has strayed too far from the Constitution and the vision of the Founding Fathers to be able to truly say the United States is still a democracy.

"If we make peaceful revolution impossible, then we make violent revolution inevitable."

~ John F. Kennedy, 35th President

America's independence was created as a result of oppression and the resulting revolution against England's King George III. The nation has come full circle and returned to the very thing that caused the fight for independence in the first place. The Declaration of Independence grants the right to throw off an oppressive government and it would appear the time has come where the nation is facing a 'new' American Revolution.

PART TWO

"The price of freedom is visible not only in flag draped coffins, but in the changed emotions of returning troops and in our V.A. hospitals."

~ Jessi Winchester, Author

PART TWO

INTRODUCTION

We have explored how radically constitutional freedoms have eroded since the early presidential administrations of the fledgling nation and how the path chosen to be followed by each president impacted on the vision of the Founding Fathers. By the time of George W. Bush's presidency, freedoms guaranteed by the U.S. Constitution had eroded a bit at a time so the public wouldn't notice but the aftermath of September 11, 2001 left America in a panic over the numerous liberties that were infringed under the guise of "necessity" in order to fight terrorism. The Patriot Act ominously appropriated liberties guaranteed in the Constitution and the Military Commissions Act of 2006 along with the John Warner Defense Authorization Act of 2007 and the Insurrection Act further assisted in destroying freedoms so wisely put in place all those years ago. Time has validated that laws passed to supposedly protect citizens were actually being used against them.

No event in modern times has affected the United States more than the September 11, 2001 attack by Islamic terrorists. An open and free way of life was changed forever, as was the nation's political outlook. Terrorists hoped to create an environment of terror that would lead toward the financial and emotional collapse of the nation and America helped them with unrestrained laws and over-kill constraint.

Part Two examines laws passed since the World Trade Center was attacked, whose reason was always under the pretext of "fighting terrorism" – but was it really?

We also analyze documents and policies that have been put in place to create a New World Order, a way of life the Founding Fathers could never imagine but to which America is systemically advancing.

Americans had no problem with putting tools in place that would give the government 'prudent' ability to fight terrorism but government went overboard after 9/11 in passing laws that were so oppressive and freedom intrusive that they serve to do exactly what the terrorists had hoped…end the open and free society of the United States. A few of these overly broad and Draconian laws follow. They impact America's freedom in frightening ways and have helped lead the nation to the crisis it now faces.

Chapter 10

REFLECTIONS

". . .I will support and defend the Constitution of the United States against all enemies, foreign and domestic . . ."
~ Oath of Office
U.S. Code, Section 502

"It can't be repeated too often that the Constitution is a limitation on the *government*, not on private individuals - that it does not prescribe the conduct of the private individual, only the conduct of the government - that it is not a charter for government power, but a charter of citizen protection against the government."
~ Ayn Rand, Author

"Just because you do not take an interest in politics doesn't mean politics won't take an interest in you."
~ Pericles [430 B.C.]

"The evils of government are directly proportional to the tolerance of the people."
~Frank Kent, Artist

"The American people will never knowingly adopt Socialism, but under the name of Liberalism they will adopt every fragment of the Socialist program until Americans will one day be a Socialist nation without knowing how it happened."

~ Norman Thomas
6-time Presidential candidate of the Socialist
Party who retired from politics when Democrat
Franklin Roosevelt ran on the same platform
and won.

"The price of apathy toward public affairs is to be ruled by evil men."

~ Plato, Greek Philosopher

"The world is a dangerous place to live, not because of the people who are evil, but because of the people who don't do anything about it."

~ Albert Einstein

"Whoever wishes to foresee the future must consult the past; for human events ever resemble those of preceding times."

~ Machiavelli; 1469-1527
Italian Political Philosopher

Chapter 11

NEW WORLD ORDER

"To achieve One World Government it is necessary to remove from the minds of men their individualism, their loyalty to family traditions, and national identification."

~ Brock Chisholm
Former director of UN World Health Organization

The very term 'New World Order' conjures up a vision that is shrouded in confusion to the average American yet we are hearing about it more and more. What exactly *is* the New World Order, what does it mean to the every day American, and why does it strike fear in the heart of freedom loving citizens everywhere?

Confusion exists because there have been two versions of NWO since President Woodrow Wilson first mentioned it in his 'Fourteen Points' speech in 1918. The speech contained fourteen topics to be discussed at a post-World War I peace conference but a more sinister twist was attributed to the term NWO when it was learned Wilson's close advisor, Col. Edward House, led the team that developed the fourteen points. House was a known follower of socialism and an advocate of the Karl Marx philosophy so a cloud of distrust and suspicion surrounded the New World Order concept.

Regardless of the harmless spin usually put on various references to NWO over the years, there has been too much evidence pointing to the fact there is indeed disturbing elements to the objectives of this endeavor.

Simply put, New World Order (NWO) is acknowledged to be a global dominance by an elitist class of business and political leaders for economic protection that would immeasurably restrict the individualism and freedom of the common person. Among some of the prominent families said to be key members are the Rockefellers, DuPonts, Rothschilds, J.P. Morgan, and Bushs as well as international organizations such as the U.N., World Bank, NATO, and the European Union.[1]

The NWO vision is one of a global society managed by an elite central government whose goal over time is a world currency, world bank, world government, world police force, and world courts. Those who publicly portray the NWO plan as a global domination are discredited by the politically pandering mainstream media as 'conspiracy theory nuts' but proof of the NWO existence and intentions can no longer be denied or ignored.

The background and beginnings of the NWO are complex but it is important to look at some of the highlights in order to better understand what is being formulated since it continues to gain strength as it spans generation to successive generation.

The world view began with leaders in various walks of life who felt contempt for the masses they viewed as being below their station in life and who felt it was their birthright to establish a world government ruled only by handpicked individuals to advance their goal of promoting and protecting their many economic assets. The Council on Foreign Relations [CFR][2] is a Rockefeller financed foreign policy pressure group and former CFR Chairman John McCloy admitted they had been handpicking individuals through networking the Ivy League schools even prior to the 1940s.

Colonel Edward M. House[3] was an author and politician who supported the Karl Marx philosophy and socialism as well as being a close advisor to President Woodrow Wilson. He was pivotal in the secret meeting of bankers and politicians, which created the Federal Reserve in 1913. While neither federal nor reserve, this shifted the power to create money from the U.S. government to a private group of bankers and is undoubtedly the largest producer of debt in the world. A few years later Col. House arranged a meeting of Socialists to reorganize the Institute of International Affairs into the Council of Foreign

Affairs, which endorsed a One World Government and is responsible for hand picking leaders.

The League of Nations[4] was the first attempt at a New World Order and by the 1930s publications were openly advocating this concept. During this era, author George Counts encouraged teachers to *"… reach for power and then make the most of your conquest"* in influencing attitudes, hearts, and minds of coming generations to embrace a form of social state. The final meeting was held on April 18, 1946 at which time the League of Nations was disbanded.

The Second World War set the stage for 'peacekeeping forces' that were continued on to future conflicts such as the Korean and Vietnam wars. Flare-ups all over the globe are deliberately planned, encouraged and even abetted in order to provide an excuse for eventually sending these military forces to nearly every nation on the planet, thus ensuring global control. This is accomplished one skirmish at a time so focus is deflected from the ultimate goal.

It doesn't seem to be a coincidence that George H.W. Bush engaged Saddam Hussein in conflict but the principle subject escaped capture, or that George W. Bush declared war on Osama bin Laden with that target also escaping capture. Could it be that both these proponents of NWO orchestrated each campaign to promote conflict and catastrophe in a foreign nation that would result in placement of peacekeeping troops and help establish global control…one country at a time?

In 1945 when the U.N. Charter became effective, Senator Glen Taylor (D-Idaho) introduced Senate Resolution 183 favoring creation of a world republic including an international police force. In 1949 the contemptible Senator introduced a senate resolution to create a world government constitution. The Senate Foreign Relations Subcommittee in the form of Resolution 66 again proposed it in 1950. During this committee meeting international financier James Warburg testified that, *"The question is only whether world government will be achieved* **by consent or by conquest**.*"*

In 1948 behavioral psychologist B.F. Skinner proposed that society should move toward a more perfect order where children are raised by the state rather than by their parents. His ideas were widely implemented by educators in the last half of the 20th Century.

The same year, U.S. educators published a preliminary draft of a World Constitution which included a 'Chamber of Guardians' to enforce world law, a 'Preamble' demanding all arms be turned over to the world government, and the right to seize private property for federal use. Today, one of the most powerful and influential unions is that of the teachers and we have only to look at law enforcement's search and seizure policy to see the writing on the wall.

In a speech to the American Bar Association in Kentucky, former Secretary of State John Foster Dulles disgracefully stated in 1952 that, "...*treaty laws can override the Constitution...and they can cut across the rights given to the people by their Constitutional Bill of Rights.*" GOP Sen. John Bricker proposed an amendment that no treaty could supersede the Constitution but it failed by just *one* vote.

The Bilderberger Society[5] was established in 1954. Its members are comprised of international bankers and politicians who meet secretly on an annual basis to work toward a NWO. Another secret fraternity considered the most powerful organization in America is the Order of Skull & Bones.[6] Based out of Yale University and dating back to the late 1800s, this elitist group boasts leading members of America's intelligence community as well as highest ranking members of the U.S. government who feel it is their 'right' to control world affairs. Former President George H.W. Bush was highly influenced by the concept of NWO which is the basis of Skull & Bones' philosophy and belief system and even talked about it in his Inauguration address - **AFTER taking an oath to uphold the Constitution**! He again praised the NWO concept in his 1991 State of the Union address.

Hypocritically, those with the most insistent rhetoric promoting a new world with no private property and no individual freedoms are the very ones whose personal lifestyles reek of extravagant excess, self-indulgence and a lust for power. Intended global policy makers have never endured real poverty yet they are determined to dictate how the poor should live.

Few have spoken up in protest but in 1954, Senator William Jenner objected saying, "... *the path to total dictatorship in the U.S. can be laid by strictly legal means…outwardly we have a Constitutional government. We have operating within our government and political system, another body representing another form of government, a bureaucratic elite which believes our Constitution is outmoded. This group has its own local political support organizations, its own pressure groups, its own vested interests, its foothold within our government, and its own propaganda apparatus.*" Those are really terrifying words from one who would know and yet, all these years later, there has been little outcry from the public.

Document Number 7277 titled "Freedom From War" presented by the U.S. State Department in 1961 unveiled a plan to fully arm the U.N. Peace Force while totally disarming all nations. The ultimate goal of this strategy was to ensure no state would have the military power to challenge the progressively strengthened U.N. Peace Force.

Nelson Rockefeller pledged in his 1968 presidential campaign that if elected he would work toward creation of a 'new world order.' Another member of the Rockefeller family, international financier David Rockefeller, a member of the Bilderberg Society and chairman of the Rockefeller controlled Chase Manhattan Bank, established the Trilateral Commission in 1973.[7] It is disturbing to note that the Trilateral Commission which plays a considerable role in the development and expansion of the NWO is referred to as the Trilateral Commission/World Shadow Government. The commission is a private partnership between the ruling classes of North America, Western Europe, and Japan for the purpose of creating a worldwide economic power superior to the political governments of the involved nation-states. By so doing, they felt they would rule the future. Rockefeller controlled every aspect and selected the commission's first director, author and Columbia University Professor Zbigniew Brzezinski, who later became the National Security Advisor to President Jimmy

Carter. Brzezinski made it clear he felt it was necessary for the upper class to band together to protect its interests and make sure political leaders were put in power in developed nations who would protect the financial interests of elitists. To that end, Jimmy Carter was invited to join because Rockefeller and Brzezinski felt he was a liberal with presidential promise who would be willing to further their aims and cooperate with their directives. With 'a little help from his friends,' Carter became president in 1976, appointing numerous Trilateralists to key policymaking positions and becoming the ultimate puppet for the Trilateral agenda.

At a Bilderberg Society meeting in Germany in 1991, David Rockefeller revealed the extent to which elitist proponents of the Trilateral Commission and NWO control mainstream media. In a speech, Rockefeller thanked the Washington Post, New York Times, Time Magazine, and others "... *whose directors have attended our meetings and respected their promises of discretion for almost forty years. It would have been impossible for us to develop our plan for the world if we had been subjected to the light of publicity during those years.*"

On a Cable News Network program the same year, former CIA Director Stansfield Turner said this about Iraq, "*We have a much bigger objective...the U.N. is deliberately intruding into the sovereignty of a sovereign nation. This is a marvelous precedent to be used in all countries of the world...*"

The U.N. advances the NWO plan by imposing fact-finding missions upon nations in hostility or conflict. These 'inquiries' often take on the menacing posture of an international tribunal that should not be tolerated by **any** sovereign state. While most countries are intimidated and acquiesce, Israel engaged in a tense showdown with the U.N. over the fighting at the Jenin refugee camp in 2002 because they felt their rights were being trampled and ignored. They refused to allow the U.N. fact-finders to arrive, or to cooperate with their mission. The right of sovereign states to decide their own matters rather than be dictated to by global 'parents' was at issue. It is crucial for countries to stand strong against global interference and in defense of national freedom as opposed to a NWO.

NAFTA [North American Free Trade Agreement] is a victory for proponents of a new world order because it opens the border between Mexico, Canada, and the United States for free trade. American companies can manufacture their products outside U.S. borders and then return them to the United States with little or no imposed tariff, to sell the product at a tremendous profit. Trilateralist Winston Lord delivered a speech in 1992 where he stated, *"To a certain extent, we are going to have to yield some of our sovereignty...under NAFTA."* He went on to become Assistant Secretary of State in the Clinton administration. Another proponent of NAFTA, Trilateralist Henry Kissinger, wrote in the L.A. Times in 1993 that NAFTA *"is not a conventional trade agreement but the architecture of a new international system...a first step toward a New World Order."*

By the arrival of the 21st Century, the characterization of 'New World Order' had taken on a negative connotation and become a political liability as a result of criticism and opposition to the plan. The phrase was replaced by the new "politically correct" expression 'global governance.' <u>Regardless of what it is called, it still stands for the elimination of the U.S. Constitution and our free and open society.</u>

* * * *

It's pretty hard to fight 75 years of cunning development by the most powerful people on the planet. Progress toward this ominous goal has been carefully orchestrated over several decades in an effort to quietly put everything in place for global dominance with the least amount of awareness or resistance. Separation of classes with the huge gap between rich and poor and total elimination of the middle class will be devastating, damning, and permanent. Attempting to behead the monster at this juncture in time will not be an easy task as a majority of those in a position to rein in this treason are the very ones involved in perpetrating it. Oppositionists are getting a late start - perhaps too late. The magnitude of this plan is almost beyond comprehension but we **must** take off the blinders quickly if we dare to hope freedom will survive.

Capitalist countries are being lulled into a false sense of security. Those behind the NWO count on apathy and silence from the general public in order to succeed. The challenge for each freedom loving resident of this planet is to take this situation seriously and not discard or ignore it as just another conspiracy theory.

In this time of unrest, it behooves every citizen to become a student of the political scene to the extent that they examine, evaluate, and question every day political activity to determine what is outside the boundaries of freedom. When one realizes the extent of this threat to our very way of life - and to the lives of those that follow us - the next obvious step is to share that information with others and establish organized opposition.

Officials, from local law enforcement to the President of the United States, take an Oath of Office that includes a promise to uphold and defend the Constitution and to protect citizens against enemies, foreign and domestic. Bureaucrats in droves are trampling that oath and placing freedom in harm's way. It is time to start **demanding** – in great numbers – that those who commit treason by not upholding their pledge to the American public, be immediately removed and charges instituted against them. Only when there are consequences and leaders are held accountable will change come about.

Former Homeland Security Director Tom Ridge announced during his tenure that the changes his office has made in the way of life for American citizens as a result of 9/11 are **permanent** – exactly as many freedom fighters predicted.

If more terrorism is expected on American soil, why then do Chief Executives refuse to close the borders and keep the enemy at bay? What do they have to gain by keeping the borders open even during a time of great danger and allowing hordes of immigrants to overtax the nation's resources to the point of becoming a Third World country? Becoming vulnerable to global domination is one scenario. An additional possibility is that acts of terrorism on American soil can only serve to further panic Americans and cause them to hand over any remaining freedoms in exchange for falsely perceived safety.

The most realistic answer can be found in the 2005 Security and Prosperity Partnership[8] agreement between Mexico, the U.S., and Canada for a new borderless 'North American Union.' All situations serve to enhance and advance the NWO plan, however.

Why has global dominance not happened already? For America, the answer is because the U.S. Constitution, battered and circumvented as it is, is still the Law of the Land. The First Amendment still confers the right to free speech. As long as opposing opinions can still be heard on talk radio, and selected books are not banned, and authors who criticize the government are not rounded up and sent to detainment camps, and those participating in dissident gatherings are not arrested, global dominance cannot take place.

The First Amendment was vastly threatened by HR 1955, a bill titled Violent Radicalization and Homegrown Terrorism Prevention Act of 2007[9] that would have classified those who complain about government policies as 'homegrown terrorists' and allow for their prosecution without due process. While this bill never became law, the mere fact it was proposed is frightening and leaves open the possibility it could be reintroduced at a later date.

The First Amendment is also threatened by proposed changes to the Fairness Doctrine, which if passed would substantially silence conservative 'talk' programs by requiring an equal number of liberal 'talk' programs and/or equal time for both conservative and liberal viewpoints during any specific program. Liberal 'talk' programs have customarily not proliferated because they simply are not successful but if liberal viewpoints fail to equal the number of conservative viewpoints, conservative programs would be cut by that amount. Issues regarding constitutionality are certain to be lodged against this measure as it 'censors' free speech. It equates to a sneaky way of censoring what the public hears and any threat to the First Amendment is a threat to freedom but a triumph for the NWO.

As long as the Second Amendment survives and the country is armed, it is not possible for global dictatorship to be implemented. That is why there is such a push to disarm the planet. **Once people are incapable of rising up and defending themselves – they are helpless against total control.**

The battle against global dominance is daunting but we have tasted freedom and hopefully we will not allow it to be taken from us without a fight.

Chapter 12

REFLECTIONS

"Power always thinks it has great soul and vast views beyond the comprehension of the weak; and that it is doing God's service, when it is violating all divine laws."
~ John Adams
2nd President of the U.S.

"Law is often but the tyrant's will and always so when it violates the right of an individual."
~ Thomas Jefferson
3rd President of the U.S.

"The marvel of all history is the patience with which men and women submit to burdens unnecessarily laid upon them by their government."
~ William H. Borah; Author

"The essence of government is power; and power, lodged as it must be in human hands, will ever be liable to abuse."
~ James Madison
4th President of the U.S.

"The state calls its own violence 'law,' but that of the individual 'crime.'
~ Max Stirner
German Author; 1806-1856

"The difference between dictatorship and democracy is that dictatorships originate from the top down, democracies from the bottom up."
~ Herbert Hoover
31st President of the U.S.

"I'm afraid, based on my own experience, that fascism will come to America in the name of national security."
~Jim Garrison,
Former New Orleans D.A.
Prosecutor, JFK Assassination Investigation

"The only thing necessary for the triumph of evil is for good men to do nothing."
~ Edmund Burke
English statesman and author; 1729 – 1797

Chapter 13

EXECUTIVE ORDERS

Ever wonder why more and more prisons are being built but so many remain empty? Presidential executive orders certainly make it clear. Under a 'national emergency,' these prisons would become relocation camps for American citizens run by F.E.M.A. [Federal Emergency Management Agency].

The FEMA website is quite candid about the fact that for the past 15 years presidential executive orders authorize the agency to exercise powers akin to those implemented during World War II by Nazi Germany should a 'national emergency' be declared.

It is frightening to realize that a president - *one person* - can interpret what is an emergency and start the ball rolling that would separate families and ruin millions of lives. But executive orders already written and part of law do exactly that.

Copies of the orders are available from the Federal Register in Washington, D.C. If/when enacted, these orders would completely do away with the Constitution, render it totally worthless, and it would cease to exist.

Under the incredibly powerful F.E.M.A., the following executive orders could be **immediately** enforced:

E.O. 10995 - "...provides for the seizure of all communications media in the United States."

E.O. 10997 - "...provides for the seizure of all electric power, petroleum, gasoline, fuels and minerals, both public and private."

E.O. 10998 – "...provides for the seizure of all food supplies and resources, public and private, and ALL farms, lands, and equipment."

E.O. 10999 – "...provides for the seizure of all means of transportation, including personal cars or vehicles of any kind, and control of all highways, seaports, and waterways."

E.O. 11000 – "...provides for the **seizure of ALL American people** for work forces under federal supervision, including splitting up of families if the government has need to."

E.O. 11001 – "...provides for government seizure of all heath, education and welfare functions."

E.O. 11002 – "...designates the postmaster general to operate a national registration of all persons." **[This is where families would be split up, as people would be ordered to report to the local post office to be separated and assigned to a new area].**

E.O. 11003 – "...provides for the government to take over all airports and aircraft; commercial, public and private."

E.O. 11004 – "...provides for the Housing and Finance Authority to relocate communities, designate areas to be abandoned, and establish new locations and populations."

E.O. 11005 – "...provides for the government to take over railroads, inland waterways, and public storage facilities."

E.O. 11051 – "...FEMA has complete authorization to put the above orders into effect in time of increased international tension or economic or financial crisis."

E.O. 11490 – "...provides absolute dictatorial presidential control over all U.S. citizens, businesses, and churches during a State of Emergency where martial law is declared."

E.O. 12148 – FEMA would take over under conditions of insurrection, or a national financial crisis.

E.O. 12656 – "...provides for a declaration of a State of Emergency during natural disaster, military attack, technological emergency, or other emergencies that threaten the national security of the United States. It allows total and unquestioned federal takeover of every local police enforcement agency as well as local price fixing and wages and forbids reassignment of personal financial assets within or outside of the United States."

E.O. 12919 – "…allows various Cabinet officials to take over all aspects of the U.S. economy during a State of Emergency, at the direction of the president."

E.O. 13010 – "…allows FEMA to take control over all government agencies."

President Nixon combined all of the above orders into E.O. 11490 which would be implemented if a national emergency were to be declared by the president. Another terrorist attack on U.S. soil could present the perfect circumstances for a power hungry president to become a dictator.

President Clinton signed E.O. 12919 in June 1994, which spells out the extent of power allocated to FEMA. Included among those powers are confiscation of all property – including firearms - from the American people, their relocation, and assignment to 'labor camps.' FEMA would work in conjunction with the U.N. and American troops are already being brainwashed and conditioned to assist U.N. forces against their own fellow citizens, family, friends, and neighbors.

An eventual 'international emergency' would be all that's needed to implement the above orders and turn America into a total dictatorship. George H.W. Bush even signed an executive order in 1989 permitting FEMA to build internment camps.[1] Yes, you heard correctly. There are currently 43 primary camps capable of holding up to 100,000 citizens and hundreds of secondary facilities including countless state prisons that have been completed but hold no prisoners.

A call from the president to the attorney general could result in the issuance of millions of arrest warrants to round up patriots deemed a threat to total control. Citizens on the 'politically incorrect' list would find themselves residing in the internment camps that have already been set up by FEMA.

An existing FEMA operation would use ATF, national guard, active duty soldiers, and local police to make house-to-house sweeps to seize all guns and food.

On October 1, 1994 the United Nations took control of underground satellite tracking facilities within the U.S. that have the ability to focus a camera on a person's property to the point of being able to read the street number on their door. Modern technology and evil intent by top leaders in America's own government have made it impossible for innocent, law abiding citizens to live without fear.

Executive orders were created, signed, and placed in the Federal Register in Washington, D.C. without fanfare or public notice. While they are technically public knowledge, one would not be aware of their existence if they were not a watchdog of public policy. These sinister orders are a deception and betrayal of the U.S. Constitution and the American people by the occupant of the Oval Office.

U.S. military is comprised of American fathers, husbands, brothers, and sons. Washington would turn them into jackbooted thugs with implementation of current Executive Orders. Relatives, friends, and neighbors would be the ones stomping through the streets, surrounding neighborhoods, and breaking down doors.

Never in our darkest nightmares could we have imagined the enemy could be our own countrymen.

Chapter 14

REFLECTIONS

"The Patriot Act: Turning citizens into suspects since 2001"
~ Bumper Sticker

"Voice or no voice, the people can always be brought to the bidding of the leaders. That is easy. All you have to do is tell them they are being attacked and denounce the pacifists for lack of patriotism and exposing the country to danger. It works the same way in any country."
~ Herman Goering
Nazi Lieutenant in Hitler's Regime

"The true danger is when liberty is nibbled away, for expedience, and by parts."
~ Edmund Burke 1729-1797
English statesman and author

"As Americans we must always remember that we all have a common enemy, an enemy that is dangerous, powerful, and relentless. I refer, of course, to the federal government."
~ Dave Barry, Pulitzer Prize Winner
Miami Herald Journalist

"The whole aim of practical politics is to keep the populace alarmed (and hence clamorous to be led to safety) by menacing it with an endless series of hobgoblins, all of them imaginary."
~ H.L. Mencken
Political Journalist, 1880-1956

"I know what I'm fit for. I can command a body of men in a rough way; but I am not fit to be President."
~ Andrew Jackson
7th President of the United States

"A state of war only serves as an excuse for domestic tyranny."
~Alexander Solzhenitsyn
Russian Dissident

"A tyrant is always stirring up some war or other, in order that the people may require a leader."
~ Plato

Chapter 15

USA PATRIOT ACT

HR 3162 / Public Law 107-56

Full Title: Uniting and Strengthening America by Providing Appropriate Tools Required to Intercept and Obstruct Terrorism

> *"If tyranny and oppression come to this land, it will be in the guise of fighting a foreign enemy."*
>
> ~ James Madison,
> 4th President of the U.S.

After the unspeakable events of September 11, 2001 when zealot terrorists tried to destroy the very fabric of America, the USA Patriot Act was ramroded through Congress and became law only 45 short days later. In a rush of emotion, anger, and panic, the country's own government did more damage to America's free and open society than any terrorist could have ever accomplished.

The assault on America changed life in dramatic and permanent ways but the Constitution and the very core of the American way of life was under greater attack by its own leaders with the alarming HR 3162, the Anti-terrorism Act of 2001.

Emotions of the 9/11 moment led residents to allow government to unnecessarily strip them of too many personal liberties under the guise of 'national security' and under the pretext that giving up freedoms would make Americans 'safer.' The United States' own government did as much damage as the terrorists when lawmakers rushed into passing the massive liberty invasive proposal of HR 3162. As too often happens, what starts out as good and necessary intent is too often abused with time. Years after 9/11, history has proven this to be true.

Benjamin Franklin was so right when he said, *"Those who would sacrifice liberty for safety will have neither liberty nor safety."*

The most astonishing aspect to come out of the 9/11 devastation was the short amount of time it took for the Department of Justice to generate the colossal anti-terrorism bill. The slow moving wheels of bureaucracy are legendary, yet this enormous volume was passed in only 45 short days after the attack. It is simply mind boggling to think it was even possible in that timeframe and begs the question, "Was this in the works prior to 9/11?" That is a legitimate conclusion considering the magnitude of the undertaking.

Without question it is important to provide <u>reasonable</u> tools and resources needed for fighting the enemy and protecting the homeland. HR 3162 however, wound up containing many non-related terrorism bills that had been unable to pass on their own merits. Bureaucrats hoped to 'hide' them in HR 3162 and rush it through Congress before private agendas were detected. Other sections amended laws that were already on the books to grant undue expansion in the rushed anti-terrorism bill.

The Bush administration wanted permission to vastly expand liberty intrusive procedures under the pretext it was 'necessary' under the circumstances in which the United States found itself so they played on the emotions of the public with fear tactics in an effort to get their agendas passed immediately through the Anti-terrorism Act of 2001. U.S. Attorney General John Ashcroft pushed the envelope when he addressed the Senate Judiciary Committee on behalf of the bill, telling his audience they would be 'unpatriotic' if they didn't pass the bill immediately. Republican staffers ordered cameras out of the hearing room when free speech and civil liberty representatives were to testify. It is disturbing that top leaders didn't want ALL sides of the issues heard publicly or that lawmakers lacked concern that such broadly expanded authority would be a direct conflict with citizens' civil liberties. Congress should have raised questions about the heavy handed push to pass these proposals so quickly without allowing time for lawmakers to fully read the legislation and give it calm, sufficient, and prudent review as well as giving it the full, deliberate, and open debate that should have taken place before such a bill was passed.

Not a single right should have been waived by law abiding citizens. Civil liberties should absolutely **not** have to be given up in a quest to track terrorists. The public was duped into believing it was necessary and their patriotic duty, when in fact, compromising the Constitution and invading personal liberties is absolutely unconscionable in a free society. **By allowing government to legislate away freedoms in the name of 'national security,' the terrorists have won because they have been successful in diminishing freedom and an open society.** Means were already available for tracking terrorists so HR 3162 should never have invaded the rights of innocent law abiding citizens. Fighting terrorism should never hamper freedom. Never.

Washington bureaucrats told the public that the war policy would require that they give up some of their rights and privacies 'for the national good' and to be 'safe.' A red flag is certain to go up for any freedom loving individual who hears that statement. History has shown that 'necessity' almost always opens the door to tyranny and abuse. America is a country that has the capability to track terrorists without invading the constitutional rights of millions of innocent citizens. That's what search warrants are for. The Fourth Amendment decrees that warrants were put in place to provide government agencies with the tools necessary to apprehend criminals while protecting the civil rights of the innocent at the same time. Even during times of extreme emergency, America's judiciary system must be vigilant and warrants must remain the legal procedure that separates the legitimate job of hunting criminals from outright tyranny.

The president was given broad power to enact whatever HE deemed 'necessary.' Does this create too much power for just one branch of office? How are individual rights of innocent law abiding citizens to be protected against potential abuses of power? Who will be the nation's watchdog to protect its citizens against abuse? Who will protect the rights and liberties guaranteed to innocent citizens under the Constitution? If one looks back on the history of the country, there have always been those in power who took advantage of wartime to further restrict freedom and destroy the rights of the individual. To see a democratic way of life crumble would give terrorists their greatest victory. It must be the first goal of America's leaders to deny them that pleasure.

HR 3162 was presented as an emergency war time measure. Similar measures were enacted during World War I and World War II. For instance, the Victory Tax of World War II was a 'temporary' tax on wages to help finance the war effort. It was to cease upon the end of hostilities with Japan but remains today in the form of federal income tax. Emergency powers enacted during those times were allowed to continue into peacetime. Are the mistakes made during those eras destined to be repeated by unjustifiably restricting liberties and then finding ourselves in a permanent state of freedom restriction once peace is restored?

HR 3162 as passed was a victory for terrorism and a defeat for individual freedom from which residents of this nation may never recover. America's military has been sent to fight for freedom. They deserve to return to a land whose leaders will defend that freedom with equal passion at home.

HR 3162, or the USA Patriot Act, was introduced in the House of Representatives on October 23, 2001. It passed the House on October 24, 2001 and passed the Senate the following day, October 25, 2001. President George W. Bush signed it into law 24-hours later on October 26, 2001. HR 3162 or Public Law 107-56 swept through Congress in a stunningly brief amount of time giving concern that it was passed with little or no prudent review and debate for such an important liberty invasive bill. Rep. John Conyers, Jr. (D-MI) even alleged that most senators simply don't have time to read bills before voting on them and that most had not read the Patriot Act.

The purpose of the Act was to increase law enforcement's ability to search telephone, e-mail communications, financial, medical, and other records, expand the definition of terrorism to include domestic terrorism which would greatly expand law enforcement's powers, and various other issues, which tended to be overbroad and have been criticized for weakening or eliminating various civil liberties and even breaching the Constitution.

The Patriot Act changed a number of U.S. laws but several of the sections within the Patriot Act were found by the courts to be unconstitutional so changes to the Act via "reauthorization bills" eliminated or amended the intent and language of those sections and expanded the "sunset" date for others.

Following is a brief overview of the ten Titles contained in the Patriot Act and mention of a few of the most freedom prohibiting sections within those Titles.

Title I: Contains miscellaneous bills proposed prior to the Patriot Act that couldn't pass on their own merits or didn't really fit in other sections of the Act so they were 'warehoused' into Titles I and X. Some provisions altered already existing laws.

Title II: Enhanced Surveillance Procedures. Federal wiretaps operate under two distinctly different statutes. One statute is the Foreign Intelligence Surveillance Act – or FISA – which was enacted in 1978. A secret, seven-judge court in Washington, D.C. authorizes extremely secret wiretaps, which give broad surveillance powers to the Feds. Anti-terrorist wiretaps would fall under FISA and the bill seeks expansion of FISA's power. The other statute is the Wiretap Act, which is used for ordinary crimes and is completely unrelated to terrorism and is extremely damaging to a free society. While it's possible the Wiretap Act *could* be used in a terrorist investigation, in its present form wiretapping is authorized for around 100 common crimes ranging from a rare homicide investigation all the way down to student loan fraud. Three-fourths of wiretaps relate to drug activity. The anti-terrorist bill wanted to expand its power to vastly increase federal government's ability to conduct surveillance of the reading habits and correspondence of the average American citizen without their knowledge or permission. If the government is investigating a specific person suspected of terrorism, that would be acceptable – but to randomly invade the rights and privacy of innocent citizens is NOT acceptable and has nothing whatsoever to do with terrorism.

Another surveillance provision allows federal courts to use surveillance illegally conducted by foreign governments who often conduct illegal electronic surveillance of American citizens by using facilities housed in consulates or embassies. A foreign government can violate American wiretapping laws and be protected by the rule of secrecy that applies to confidential informants. This means our judicial system could get around illegal wiretapping by U.S. agencies by using foreign information gained illegally – in exchange for the U.S. illegally wiretapping foreign citizens. This mutual collusion benefits both.

Title II altered the U.S.C. Title 18 Criminal Code to *demand* that cable companies and Internet Service Providers disclose customer information upon demand. Subpoenas expanded the required information to include name, address, telephone number, billing records, length of service, IP address, payment method, bank account data, and credit card numbers. Objections cite the provision as unconstitutional in that it violates the Fourth Amendment of the U.S. Constitution and gives the FBI 'carte blanc' to violate the communications privacy of countless innocent Americans. A 'gag' was originally included that would have prevented companies from notifying customers that the government was looking at their records but was later amended to prevent a delayed notification in order to prevent potential abuse by law enforcement agencies.

Section 206 - Roving Wiretaps - was one of the most contentious provisions in the Act. The invasive surveillance tactics of this section were expanded to include addressing and routing information, ignoring the fact that e-mail or web addresses often contain additional personal data in the address information. The December 31, 2005 'sunset' expiration date of this section was changed to December 31, 2009 by the Reauthorization Act of 2005.

Section 213 – Sneak and Peek – originally allowed surveillance to be done without notification to the target. Officers simply went in to a home or business and searched the premises without permission or prior notice. When done, the target was never told they had been there because their "delayed notification" procedure enabled them to never "get around to notifying" the target. Notification was changed by the Reauthorization Act of 2005 to require a period not exceeding 30 days from the execution of a search warrant. The provisions were so Draconian, however, that in September 2007 the court found it to be unconstitutional as it violated the Fourth Amendment.

Section 214 – Pen Register and Trap and Trace Authority Under FISA. Two operations called 'pen register' and 'trap and trace' were originally felt to not be a violation of the U.S. Constitution and did not require police to obtain a warrant. A pen register is a device, which records all outgoing numbers that are dialed by a particular phone. A trap and trace is an electronic device that would show all incoming phone numbers that had called a specific telephone. Judges were required to issue orders for federal use whenever a U.S. Attorney General requested as a result of a congressional statute. When originally implemented in 1979, the procedures recorded only numbers and not personal data. Expansion of that authority under the Patriot Act leaves the door open to abuse of innocent citizens, however.

Section 215 – Access to Records – allowed the government to secretly demand library records without reason to believe readers were involved in anything illegal. It had such a chilling effect on free speech that librarians were urged to get legal advise before complying with a search warrant and began keeping records only for the legally required timeframe before shredding them to avoid being forced to comply with the Feds. The sunset date for this provision was changed to December 31, 2009 by the Reauthorization Act of 2005 and amended to give expanded judicial oversight and review as well as restricting authorization to the FBI Director and Deputy Director or the

Executive Assistant Director for National Security. The collection and distribution of data under this provision was also limited under the revision and the original "gag" order was changed to allow a target to be informed of inquiry and to contact their attorney. The requirement by the FBI that they be notified of any citizen's contact with an attorney was also removed by the Reauthorization Amendments of 2006.

Title III: International Money Laundering Abatement and Anti-Terrorism Financing Act of 2001. Subtitle A focused on international money laundering; subtitle B dealt with bank secrecy and reports, and subtitle C included currency crimes. This provision tightened the record keeping and financial reporting requirements for financial institutions and blocked mergers of financial institutions under certain circumstances.

Any senior political figure suspected of financial corruption by a financial institution was to be reported as well. Subtitle C makes it a crime for any person to conceal $10,000 or more on their person, in their luggage, or in any other container while leaving or entering the United States and provides for forfeiture of the property.

Other provisions of Title III changed existing laws to include the formation of an Entry and Exit Data System that would use biometrics to develop tamper proof documents readable at ports of entry, an expanded foreign student monitoring program, and the development of tamper-resistant passports. Secret Service jurisdiction was also expanded.

Title IV: Protecting the Border. Subtitle A addressed the northern Canadian border; subtitle B concentrated on enhanced immigration provisions; and subtitle C set forth the preservation of immigration benefits for victims of terrorism. This provision granted the U.S. Attorney General more law enforcement and investigative power.

Title V: Removing Obstacles to Investigating Terrorism. Section 507 – Disclosure of educational records – was another contentious provision pertaining to government's ability to secure private educational records.

The most controversial provision of the Patriot Act was contained in Title V as it relates to National Security Letters (NSLs), which is a type of administrative subpoena used by the FBI, CIA, and DOD (Department of Defense). It is a demand letter instructing a person or organization to turn over records and data such as financial, health, credit, and employment on individuals without the protection of probable cause or judicial oversight or a court order and contained a gag order preventing the recipient of the letter from informing anyone that they had received a NSL. The ACLU challenged the provision on the grounds it violated the First and Fourth Amendments of the U.S. Constitution and the court declared the law unconstitutional. An attempt was made to amend the NSL law to make the letters more lawful through the reauthorization Act but even that was struck down by the court because the 'gag' order was left in place.

Title VI: Providing for Victims of Terrorism, Public Safety Officers, and Their Families. Subtitle A provided aid to families of public safety officers and subtitle B amended the 1984 Victims of Crime Act.

Title VII: Increased Information Sharing for Critical Infrastructure Protection. This provision deals with the expansion of information sharing between federal, state, and local law enforcement as it relates to responding to terrorist attacks.

Title VIII: Strengthening the Criminal Laws Against Terrorism. Section 802 alters the definition of terrorism to include the term "domestic" terrorism, which broadly encompasses numerous activities such as assassination, kidnapping, mass transportation system attacks, biological weapons use, and much more. Several areas of concern regarding the expanded definition were focused on potential abuse by law enforcement agencies of innocent every day citizens.

The most chilling and alarming language in the entire bill is the *definition* of terrorism. It is so broad, it could apply to any number of minor offenses, thereby imposing a life sentence for minor criminal activities such as destruction of government property no matter how little damage; teenagers who throw rocks through a post office window; human rights activists who vandalize government office buildings; injury to the property of a foreign government; possession, production, or transfer of biological weapons; computer fraud, theft, or extortion; interfering with a flight crew member; any threatened act of violence without financial gain; and many more non-terrorist acts. While anyone committing minor crimes should be punished, it is unfathomable to label minor, non-terrorist acts as terrorism and subject those offenders to life in prison. This overly broad definition holds too much potential for horrendous abuse.

Section 805 pertained to "material support" of terrorism, which infringed the freedom of association and therefore, violated the First Amendment. The provision prohibited "expert advise and assistance" to terrorists but proved to be so vague that citizens couldn't always determine who was a terrorist and simply working around them or socializing with them innocently would put them in harm's way. The court determined this provision could easily be abused by law enforcement upon innocent citizens and would have a chilling effect on First Amendment rights so it declared the provision unconstitutional. Congress later redefined the definitions of "material support" and "expert advise or resources" to improve the law.

Title IX: Improved Intelligence. This provision amends the National Security Act of 1947 as it relates to foreign intelligence collected under FISA. It also deals with other intelligence related matters and reports.

Title X: Miscellaneous. Section 1010 grants federal agents the power to require state and local governments to perform security functions at military installations. Section 1016 allows the take-over of water, food, and miscellaneous infrastructure.

Any anti-terrorism bill of this freedom restricting magnitude should not have been rushed into and should have received intense scrutiny accompanied by a calm eye and a view toward individual liberty and upholding the sanctity of the U.S. Constitution. Any such law should never contradict a free way of life and an open society. Never.

The American heritage was patterned on the format of representing individual rights, not enhancing the career of elected bureaucrats or expanding government control. Originally the federal government's role was very limited and the Tenth Amendment of the Constitution clearly provided for states' rights to be the primary basis for the seat of power.

Eighteenth century English statesman William Pitt identified the problem when he said, *"Necessity is the excuse for every infringement of human freedom."* We see it every day with the 'necessity' to remove guns to 'protect the children,' the 'necessity' to make every telephone in the nation wire tap ready in order to intercept and diminish drug and arms activity, the 'necessity' to track citizens with transponders to chart illegal movement, the 'necessity' to seize asset property without due process in order to send a strong message to criminals, or even the 'necessity' to require seat belts or motorcycle helmets in order to protect citizens whom the government views as 'too stupid' to make their own decisions. 'Necessity' is simply an excuse by the government to invade privacy and control lives.

The list is endless but it all adds up to the same thing; what were once private decisions are now being dictated by the government. And if we don't want to do what we are told, there is another endless list of fines, regulations, consequences, threats, and intimidations to force us into compliance.

The events of September 11, 2001 and the resulting Patriot Act have redefined America's very future but a document rushed through Congress as an emergency measure that alters the nation's way of life, should never contain freedom restricting provisions that impact upon innocent citizens and if it does, Americans should **demand their freedoms not be infringed regardless of the occasion**. For freedom to continue, people must vigilantly monitor government intentions and then stand strong for the principles of freedom.

Thomas Paine articulately summed up the legacy of those who have gone before us when he said, *"Those who expect to reap the blessings of freedom must undergo the fatigue of supporting it."*

The nation's forefathers had security but they valued liberty more and proved it when they put their very lives on the line by signing the Declaration of Independence.

We have come a long way since the establishment of our Republic but our flag is stained with the blood of human sacrifice. Those before us gave up so much to preserve our liberty and freedom so we must not dishonor their solemn commitment to our future by abandoning our past - - or our responsibility to continue their vision.

Chapter 16

REFLECTIONS

"A free people ought not only to be armed and disciplined, but they should have sufficient arms and ammunition to maintain a status of independence from any who might attempt to abuse them, which would include their own government."
~ George Washington
1st President of the U.S.

"Courage is fear holding on a minute longer."
~ General George Patton, Jr.

"We Americans have no commission from God to police the world."
~Benjamin Harrison
23rd President of the U.S.

"Let us turn away from the fanatics of the far left and the far right...those who pour venom into our nation's bloodstream."
~ Lyndon Baines Johnson
36th President of the U.S.

"Tyranny, like hell, is not easily conquered. What we obtain too cheap, we esteem too lightly: it is dearness only that gives everything its value."
~ Thomas Paine, Founding Father

"It is foolish and wrong to mourn the men who died. Rather, we should thank God that such men lived."
~ General George Patton, Jr.

"A tyrant is always stirring up some war or other, in order that the people may require a leader."
~ Plato

"What's missing in America are the leaders of the past."
~ U.S. General Norman Swartzkoff

"The cry has been that when war is declared, all opposition should be hushed. A sentiment more unworthy of a free country could hardly be propagated."
~William Ellery Channing
Unitarian Pastor

Chapter 17

MILITARY COMMISSIONS ACT OF 2006

Public Law 109-366

"If the Military Commissions Act is passed, it will grant the President the privilege of kings."

~ Michael Ratner
Center for Constitutional Rights

George W. Bush struggled to paint a heroic picture of his legacy but passage of the odious Military Commissions Act of 2006[1] only served to mire him further in a legacy of deep shame.

The 2006 U.S. Supreme Court decision in the case of Hamdan v. Rumsfeld, 04-702,[2] declared tactics used by the military commissions created by the Bush administration were in violation of the U.S. Uniform Code of Military Justice as well as violating the Geneva Convention, in particular, Article 3 of the third Geneva Convention. At a later date the U.S. Constitution was also found to have been violated when the U.S. Supreme Court heard the case of Al Odah v. United States and declared on June 12, 2008 that Section 7 as it related to habeas corpus, was unconstitutional.

In defiant response to the court's ruling, Bush signed the Military Commissions Act on October 17, 2006 which not only removed any check and balance on the power of the president, it actually gave him *more* power to be the one to decide what constitutes torture and to whom and when it would be applied. The opportunity for 'selective application of the law' is tremendous.

Article 1, Section 9, paragraph 2 of the U.S. Constitution states, *"The privilege of the Writ of Habeas Corpus shall not be suspended, unless when in cases of rebellion or invasion the public safety may require it.*" Habeas corpus and warrants are the only things standing between democracy and tyranny and the nation was experiencing neither invasion nor insurrection, yet with a single arrogant and unconstitutional swipe of Bush's pen, he suspended habeas corpus. Habeas corpus grants arrested persons the ability to challenge their confinement in a court of law. The Military Commissions Act denies that right to alien detainees but claims to still allow U.S. citizens that protection. That claim has been challenged by several, including Senator Patrick Leahy who said of the Act, *"This is not just a bad bill, this is a dangerous bill."* Section 948 deleted the word "alien" and refers to "unlawful enemy combatant"…not "<u>alien</u> unlawful enemy combatant." That leaves the door open to prosecute every day American citizens as well, especially given the overly broad interpretation of "enemy combatant." The wording could allow for virtually anyone to be snatched off the street under this law.

The Act simply allows the president to do whatever he wants and cover up mistakes by declaring everything 'secret.' In essence, the president has a green light to act *outside* the law – with no check or balance.

Knowing full well there would likely be a constitutional challenge to the Act, the president enlisted the help of Congress, who obediently complied. The Act was unanimously passed according to the president's wishes, making Congress complicit in violations of detention policies.[3] Former U.S. Attorney General Alberto Gonzalez even acted as Bush's pitbull by warning federal judges, *"…not to substitute their personal views for the president's judgments in wartime."* Intimidation and censorship in demanding judges to fall into line and not question the president's judgments was inexcusable behavior by the top legal representative in the nation.

All amendments proposed before final passage of the bill were defeated, including a sunset provision by Sen. Robert Byrd, outlawing waterboard torture by Sen. Ted Kennedy, and preserving habeas corpus by Senators Arlen Specter and Patrick

Leahy. Spinelessly, Specter went on to vote in favor of the bill rather than stand strong for what was right.

A Republican Congress, elected officials, and mainstream media have all but ignored important questions about why Bush has taken such drastic and vile measures to eliminate checks on executive power as well as reduce limits on executive power by separate branches of government. It is incumbent on Congress to stand strong on behalf of the peoples' protection and be openly critical of any law that is detrimental to the personal liberties of citizens in an effort to reign in undue presidential power.

Michael Ratner of the Center for Constitutional Rights mounted a challenge to the constitutionality of the law in court but as the New York Times noted, *"Earlier Supreme Court decisions have suggested that the president and Congress acting together in the national security arena can be an all-but-unstoppable force"* so any constitutional challenge to the Act would be overwhelming.

L.A. Times Journalist Rosa Brooks wrote an article titled, "Our Torturer-in-Chief on September 22, 2006 in which she observed, *"Why is the White House suddenly so desperate to get a deal with Congress to 'clarify' Common Article 3 of the Geneva Convention and amend the War Crimes Act? The answer, of course, is that Bush knows the practices he authorized or ordered violated those laws."*

Interestingly, U.S. District Court Judge James Robertson who ruled in favor of Salim Ahmed Hamdan in the original Hamdan v. Rumsfeld case when it was heard in the District of Columbia court refused to rule in favor of Hamden on his habeas corpus challenge on December 13, 2006, citing the reason to be that Congress is now the jurisdiction to regulate combatants' access to the court system. Is it plausible intimidation and pressure from the highest levels influenced his decision?

Bush has looked America straight in the eyes and declared we don't torture. He has conducted too many problematic policies in secret. He has lied to involve us in war. Why should we believe he isn't lying when he says American citizens will be provided with habeas corpus, so we shouldn't worry? Why should we have faith we won't be snatched off the street in a mistaken identity or even for no reason at all and then denied access to an attorney, a court hearing, or even knowing if we will ever see daylight again? How are we to convince our captors we are innocent if we are denied access to an attorney? Who could we complain to if we are tortured or left in a cold unsanitary cell to fear the next hour or the next day? Are we to believe a president who completely ignores the Constitution to suspend habeas corpus has any interest at all in protecting the rights of the rest of us? Are we to believe he has not lied about his intent on how he will use this newly granted power, or on *whom* he will use it?

HR 5122(2), the John Warner Defense Authorization Act of 2007 is just as damaging and alarming as suspending habeas corpus. It was signed into law on October 17, 2006 and expands the reasons that allow the president to impose martial law and station troops anywhere in the United States he desires without consent of a state's governor. When activated, HR 5122(2) would repeal the 1878 Posse Comitatus Act, which protected local jurisdictions and even whole states from the willful intervention of corrupted or dictatorial executive branch orders being forced upon local communities by Army units in a law enforcement capacity. No more. The Bush administration has systematically gone about dismantling citizen rights, one by one.

Section 6 of the Act changed the accepted definition of "war crimes" making what previously were considered war crimes exempt so that U.S. officials who implemented or had "command responsibility for coercive interrogation techniques would be exempt from prosecution. In short, it protects government perpetrators of abuse from prosecution while acting under the guise of the "war on terror."

Rep. Ron Paul [R-Tx] introduced HR 3835, The American Freedom Agenda Act, to restore habeas corpus and repeal the Military Commissions Act of 2006. Given the oppressive political climate in which we currently live, its not surprising the bill never became law or that the 110th Congress failed to find their spine and do the right thing.

The Military Commissions Act of 2006 is just plain wrong. American citizens and Congress need to reign in this madness before its too late. Once a person is whisked off to indefinite incommunicado detention without benefit of judicial intervention, this new law allows interrogation from which most rational people would recoil. Not President Bush. He called signing the bill "a privilege." While he arrogantly smirked about the fact the bill eliminates representation by legal counsel and bars detainees from filing habeas corpus petitions to challenge their detention...those protesting the bill outside the White House were arrested for shouting, "Bush is the terrorist." So much for First Amendment rights as well.

The Military Commissions Act of 2006 works in concert with HR 5122(2) the John Warner Defense Authorization Act of 2007 and the Insurrection Act to limit the peoples' power and liberties and expand dangerous presidential power that moves the country as far from freedom and the U.S. Constitution as it can get without becoming an outright dictatorship.

Chapter 18

REFLECTIONS

"There can be no 50/50 Americanism in this country. There is room here for only 100 percent Americanism, only for those who are Americans and nothing else."
~ Theodore Roosevelt
26th President of the U.S.

"Government is not the solution to our problems, government IS the problem."
~ Ronald Reagan
40th President of the U.S.

"Tyranny is always better organized than freedom."
~ Thomas Paine, Founding Father

"Americans need to recognize that presidents are human beings, not gods, and that they must be judged and held accountable like anyone else."
~ Ronald Kessler
Author: Inside the White House

"Democracies die behind closed doors."
~ Judge Damon J. Keith
U.S. Court of Appeals, 6th Circuit
Re: George W. Bush administration

"George W. Bush has not chosen to deal honestly with the American people regarding his true agenda, where he is taking this nation, why, or how."
~ *John W. Dean; "Worse Than Watergate"*
Former White House Counsel

"He who passively accepts evil is as much involved in it as he who helps to perpetuate it."
~ Martin Luther King, Jr.,
Civil Rights Activist

"I like my beer dark, cigars strong, coffee black, bourbon straight, and politicians on the end of a rope."
~ Mark Twain

Chapter 19

THE INSURRECTION ACT

The Insurrection Act of 1807 was a set of laws that governed the president's ability to deploy troops within the United States to put down lawlessness, insurrection, and rebellion. It was designed to limit presidential power and leave decisions to state and local governments. The Insurrection Act worked in conjunction with the Posse Comitatus Act, which prevents the military from acting under the cover as a police function directed against the American people within the United States. The Act is so severe that it has been called into action only a handful of times in the past fifty years and then only with the consent of a state's governor.

The original language in the 1807 Act limited situations under which the president could deploy troops to include insurrection, domestic violence, unlawful combination, and conspiracy and could be implemented only if the president determined a state was unable to maintain order itself.

HR 5122(2), the John Warner Defense Authorization Act of 2007 was signed into law by President George W. Bush. This bill revised the original Insurrection Act to give the president unprecedented power. It left the original emergency situations in place but added additional ones such as "a natural disaster, epidemic or other serious public health emergency, terrorist attack or incident, or other condition." It allowed the president to deploy troops onto any street in the nation as well as take control of state-based National Guard units *without* the consent of a governor in order to suppress disorder during any of the stated emergencies including the vague "other conditions." Governors, military, and local law enforcement were not consulted about the sweeping changes to the Insurrection Act. Frightfully, any time an area is put under military control, it is "martial law" and HR 5122(2) permits it to do just that. Even more upsetting, Section 1076 of the HR 5122(2) bill uses the ambiguous "other conditions" term to give the president authority to order the temporary apprehension of an overly broad category of "disorderly" citizens and place them in facilities being constructed and under contract by Halliburton.

Section 334 of the HR 5122(2) bill sets forth the expanded ability of the president to declare martial law.

There has been little outcry from the public or the media regarding the ominous alterations to the Insurrection Act, in great part due to suppression of news Washington doesn't want disseminated to the public. One strong voice objected, however, and tried to make America aware of a dangerous state of affairs. Senator Patrick Leahy (D-Vt) entered into the Congressional Record his *"grave reservations"* about provisions in HR 5122(2). He stated the bill *"subverts solid, longstanding Posse Comitatus statutes"* and that using the military for law enforcement, *"goes against one of the founding tenets of our democracy. We fail our Constitution, neglecting the rights of the States, when we make it easier for the President to declare martial law and trample on local and state sovereignty."*

Because of the huge potential for abuse, Senator Leahy organized key military and law enforcement officials to testify against specific provisions in HR 5122(2). He also presented support from the nation's governors in repealing the language changes in the Insurrection Act Rider. In an unusual legislative achievement, Leahy was successful in reverting the language back to the original wording of the 1807 Insurrection Act on January 30, 2008.

Bush's administration had a long history of turning a deaf ear to the 'court of public opinion' and doing whatever he wanted to do instead. Classifying citizens who simply disagree with government policies or complain as 'terrorists' demonstrates how out-of-touch and out-of-control the federal government really is. Bureaucrats are insensitive to the needs of citizens and corruption is widespread in all levels of government. Americans have been betrayed and lied to and their rights and privacy have been invaded. Those whose responsibility it is to carry out the wishes of the people for whom they work, simply are more concerned with their own power than doing the right thing. Citizens are mad, fed up, and unwilling to tolerate more. History has shown that when a government is tyrannical, it leaves its citizens with no recourse but to resist. Washington can feel it in the air; the natives are ready to revolt and that's why those at the highest levels of government continue to try to suppress the people with bills like HR 5122(2). Only with loud protest from the pubic and leaders of principle who remain strong voices for the people, will freedom still have a chance to flourish in America.

Chapter 20

REFLECTIONS

"When the people fear the government, you have tyranny; when the government fears the people, you have liberty.
~ Thomas Jefferson
3rd President of the United States

"I believe there are more instances of the abridgement of the freedom of the people by gradual and silent encroachments of those in power than by violent and sudden usurpations."
~ James Madison
4th President of the United States

"Good people do not need laws to tell them to act responsibly, while bad people will find a way around the laws."
~ Plato

"Some candidates use 'change' to further their careers while others use their careers to further 'change.'
~ Governor Sarah Palin (Alaska)
2008 Vice Presidential Candidate

"If we make peaceful revolution impossible, then we make violent revolution inevitable."
~ John F. Kennedy
35th President of the United States

"If we have no sense of community, the American dream will wither."
~ William Jefferson Clinton
42nd President of the United States

"One of the best ways to get yourself a reputation as a dangerous citizen these days is to go about repeating the very phrases which our founding fathers used in the great struggle for independence."
~ Charles Austin Beard; 1874-1948
American Historian

"Speak the truth but ride a fast horse."
~ Cowboy motto quoted from
"The Family; The Real Story of the Bush Dynasty"
by Kitty Kelley

PART THREE

"Democracy substitutes election by the incompetent many for appointment by the corrupt few."
~ George Bernard Shaw,
Playwright

PART THREE

INTRODUCTION

Part I of *America: The Final Chapter* explored the erosion of constitutional liberties throughout the history of the American presidency and how it has contributed to the downfall of the Republic that is faced today.

Part II examined a handful of laws and documents that further pushed the United States away from the intent of the Founding Fathers and contributed to the threat to freedom now faced by the citizens of America.

Part III looks at the 2008 elections and its implications for the future of a world power. Decades of actions and decisions, good and bad, have brought America to a perilous crisis that will determine whether the nation can recover or a final chapter will be written for the nation's great experiment in democracy.

Voters typically ignore warning signs of poor character, harmful associations, precarious intent, and faulty track records to focus instead on candidate celebrity, captivating promises, or TV performances. Too often they later experience 'buyers remorse' and regret disregarding obvious clues – but of course by then it is simply too late. Bad decisions at the ballot box can result in a fatal blow to freedom. The liberal left media, a spineless Congress, and those who cast votes without proper research, demanding legitimate answers of candidates, or simply ignoring red flags must accept responsibility for that and the heavy price they may impose on <u>all</u> Americans. Only if the people find their voice and take strong action, will America survive.

Chapter 21

2008 PRESIDENTIAL CAMPAIGN CANDIDATES

****

BARACK HUSSEIN OBAMA

"Barack Obama has spent decades aiding and abetting people who hate America."

~ Thomas Sowell
Black author & columnist

Barack Hussein Obama burst into national awareness when he delivered the keynote address at the Democratic National Convention in Boston in July 2004. He was remembered for his "unity" speech where he urged, *"There is not a liberal America and a conservative America; there's the United States of America."* That appearance launched his star as a national political figure.

Obama was born on August 4, 1961 to a Black Kenyan father and a White Kansas mother who met while attending college in Hawaii. His father gave him the first name of Barack, which is an Arabic word meaning 'blessed' and was the name of Mohammad's horse. He was given a middle name of Hussein after his grandfather. Both his first and middle names are Muslim, not African.

His actual place of birth and therefore his very eligibility to become president remained under an umbrella of suspicion when Obama refused to produce his original Certificate of Live Birth, which would have shown the hospital's name and location, the signature of the delivering doctor, and the required official stamp. Enough proof exists to support the fact he was actually born in Kenya and several appeals have been filed before the U.S. Supreme Court to direct Obama to prove to the American people that he is actually in compliance with the Constitution. It would be unfathomable to even imagine a person would perpetrate such a fraud but Obama has done nothing to dispel that suspicion.

The court will never be asked to hear a more basic or important case than whether a person intentionally, deceitfully, and fraudulently fabricated his place of birth in order to run for public office and eventually, for president. Article II, Section 1, Paragraph 5 of the U.S. Constitution makes it crystal clear that, *"No person except a natural born citizen…shall be eligible to the Office of President,"* so for the court to deny that most crucial and fundamental of information to the American public simply smacks of a cover-up. It makes the public suspicious that the court is covering up an illegal act that speaks to the basic principles of the U.S. Constitution, thereby effectively silencing any voice that seeks legitimate answers under the First Amendment in the most basic of issues.

The relationship between the branches of government and the Constitution have blurred over the past 150-years to the point that the document's effectiveness is in peril. The final chapter has apparently been written for the Constitution and an open and free society when the most basic of constitutional decrees – proof that the president was born on American soil – is suppressed when questioned. A basic flaw in the separation of power of the three main branches of government exists in that the Supreme Court justices are *appointed* by the president, which makes it ripe for a cover-up of misdeeds or outright criminal behavior by a president. Obama's repeated claim of desire for a 'transparent' administration appears to have simply been campaign rhetoric because to this day he has done nothing to provide proof of his birthplace in order to ease the public's concern and put the issue to rest. If history eventually discovers the issue to have merit, then the Supreme Court, the Congress, the President himself, and the media will have lost all moral authority and the Constitution will be rendered meaningless. America's integrity will be bankrupt and those involved will have helped to write the final chapter.

When Obama was two his parents split up and Obama saw his father only one more time before a car crash took his life in 1982. His mother married an Indonesian citizen and moved Obama to Jakarta in 1967 where he attended school for nearly five years. On CNN's *Larry King Show*, Obama stated he "wasn't raised in a Muslim home," but his education during those five years remained an ambiguous and widely speculated question, which Obama seemed extremely reluctant to address. In his own autobiography, Obama openly tells of attending a Muslim school in Indonesia as well as studying the Quran. It would appear he has hidden agendas that he didn't want made public during his campaign for president, which should certainly have raised red flags for voters.

Indonesia hosts some of the most radical Islamic schools in Southeast Asia and many are alleged to be connected to terrorism. Indonesian Madrassas are funded by the Saudis who adhere to the Wahabi doctrine, the most fundamental and fanatical of Islam. The fact Obama conveniently brushed over this period in his life by saying he "gained valuable experience from living in Indonesia" but refused to discuss precisely where he went to school during those formative years spawned much speculation as to his religious philosophy during the entire scope of his campaign.

It would appear the reality gleaned from investigative reports,[1] was that Obama attended Fransiskus Assisi Catholic School for the first two years he lived in Jakarta but enrollment documents showed he enrolled as a Muslim, which may or may not have been because the school required students to list the faith of their father. After two years, Obama transferred to the affluent SDN Menteng-1 public school, which former dictator Suharto's grandchildren had attended. Akmad Solichin, vice-principal of the school, admitted most of the students were Muslim but noted that the school was public and not a Madrassa.

Obama usually glossed over his elementary school years by explaining that he returned to Hawaii to live with his maternal grandparents to attend the prestigious Punahou School from the fifth grade until he graduated from high school in 1979.

After graduating, he attended Occidental College in Los Angeles for two years but felt it was a "dead end" and transferred to Columbia University in New York City. He claimed in his book, *Dreams From My Father*, that his time at Occidental was spent doing drugs and partying.

Fox News TV aired a special on Sunday, October 5, 2008 titled, "Hannity's America: Obama's Radical Friends Exposed," in which it was disclosed that both Columbia University and Harvard Law School had been instructed not to give anyone copies of Obama's transcripts or his senior thesis. He went to great lengths to ensure his college years were clouded in secrecy. Obama shed some light into his activities during this time, however, when he disclosed in his autobiography that he attended socialist conferences at Cooper Union during his time at Columbia so it would appear his five elementary school years in Indonesia set the stage for the radical philosophies and relationships he cultivated during his college years.

He moved back to Chicago in 1985 and worked as a "community organizer" on behalf of black poverty projects. During Hannity's expose,' a panel member stated that during Obama's time at Columbia he embraced the radical revolutionary teachings of Saul Alinsky and even taught workshops on the Alinsky method during his years as an "organizer." Alinsky was a Marxist who interchanged the words 'organizing' and 'revolution.' He believed in creating enough discontent that those who feel oppressed and disillusioned would easily follow the lead of charismatic radical organizers who exude confidence and profess to understand the type of "change" that is needed. The Hannity special indicated that, to all appearances, Obama was sent to Chicago to be "tested" as a possible radical leader and to cultivate a network of like-minded influential people within the community.

While working as an 'organizer' on the south side of Chicago, one of Obama's jobs was to work in conjunction with a radical grassroots political organization called ACORN [Association of Community Organizations for Reform Now], whose purpose was to register primarily African-Americans to vote and see that they got to the polls. They were known to use forceful and often illegal tactics to bully and intimidate others to do their will and in the 2004 and 2006 elections they were found to have carried out fraudulent voter registration, rigged votes, intimidated voters, and even perpetrated scams to make voters pay to vote. According to ACORN spokesman Lewis Goldberg, Obama was invited to train the ACORN staff[2] in the late 1990s. During his presidential campaign, Obama paid Citizens Services, Inc., a subsidiary of ACORN, more than $800,000 to "enhance" organizing efforts in the primaries. ACORN was the recipient of substantial grants awarded by Obama and terrorist William Ayers who were paid Board members of the Woods Fund of Chicago, a grant-making foundation aimed at providing opportunities to impact the lives of poverty level African-Americans.

William Ayers was the unrepentant domestic terrorist who was the leader of the violent Communist Weatherman organization that carried out 30 bombings of U.S. defense and security infrastructures in the 1960s. Ayers hosted meetings in his home and contributed money during the mid-1990s to help elect Obama to the 1996 Illinois Senate seat and went on to serve with Obama as a board member of the Woods Fund of Chicago. During his presidential campaign, Obama frequently defended his association with Ayers by stating that he was only eight years old when Ayers perpetrated his terrorist acts but his argument rang hollow considering Obama was a well-informed adult when he sat on the Woods Fund board with Ayers. In yet another connection, both Ayers and Louis Farrakhan, radical leader of the Nation of Islam, live in the same posh neighborhood in Chicago as Obama.

Columbia University professor and militant activist Rashid Khalidi[3] was a former professor and director of the

Center for International Studies at the University of Chicago who was reputed to have ties to the terrorist PLO organization, a paramilitary group during the 1970s. The Khalidi family and the Obama family were close enough friends that the Khalidis babysat the Obama children and Michelle Obama attended a party in 2008 celebrating the marriage of Khalidi's daughter.

Khalidi co-founded the non-profit Woods Fund that paid Barack Obama and bombing terrorist William Ayers to serve on their board of directors. The Woods Fund awarded large grants to the Arab American Action Network, an organization for which Khalidi's wife formerly was president and which had been outspoken in their contempt toward Israel. Additionally, Mona Khalidi formerly was an English translator for terrorist Yasser Arafat's press agency.

In 1988, Obama entered Harvard Law School where he graduated with a law degree in 1991. During Sean Hannity's expose,' he presented a tape of Percy Sutton explaining how Obama was able to gain entry to the prestigious learning institution. Sutton was a black civil rights activist and attorney who represented Malcolm X and went on to serve as the Manhatten Borough president for twelve years. He was a frequent speaker at Columbia and had many friends there that could help Obama obtain entry. Dr. Khalid al-Mansoor was a principal advisor to Prince Al-Waleed Bin Talal of the Saudi Royal family and a mentor to the Black Panthers. He asked Percy Sutton to advocate on behalf of Barack Obama with his Harvard associates, which he did. While at Harvard, Obama was elected the first black president of the *Harvard Law Review* and the resulting publicity led to a contract and advance to write a book about race relations. *Dreams From My Father* was published in 1995.

Obama sought the New Party's endorsement for his 1996 state senate race and was not only successful in obtaining it but used a number of the New Party volunteers on his campaign. The New Party was a Marxist political coalition whose aim was to get leftist officials elected and set the stage for the rise of a new Marxist third party, which did not materialize because the party became non-operational in 1998.

Obama admitted in his autobiography, *Dreams From My Father*, that he attended Socialist conferences while at Columbia University so he didn't hesitate to accept the endorsement and backing of the Chicago branch of the Democratic Socialists of America during his campaign for the Illinois State Senate in 1996 and for his reelection in 1998 and 2002...yet another questionable Chicago association.

He lost the Democratic primary for U.S. House of Representatives in 2000 by a margin of two to one but nevertheless announced his candidacy for U.S. Senate in 2003. His campaign was enormously advanced by his keynote address at the 2004 Democratic National Convention and Obama went on to an overwhelming victory in the general election where, based on his senatorial votes, *The National Journal* ranked him in 2007 as the most liberal senator.

During his campaign for U.S. Senate, radical activist Rashid Khalidi held a fundraiser for Obama. Then-Chicago city council member, Dorothy Tillman, backed Obama's U.S. Senate run. Tillman was well known for her shady deals, confrontational fervor on behalf of reparation for slavery, record for corruption, and her rigid anti-white and anti-American views. According to an article in the October 30, 2006 Chicago Tribune she even ranted against Morgan Stanley, accusing them of "getting rich from investments and profits in slavery." Never mind that Morgan Stanley wasn't even formed until 1935! Regardless of her radical and irrational stand on the reparation issue, Tillman was an outspoken supporter of her longtime friend Barack Obama and in March 2007, Obama returned the favor by endorsing Tillman[4] for re-election, which she lost.

When Khalidi left Chicago in 2003 to join the Columbia University staff, the Arab American Action Network was the benefactor of a farewell party for Khalidi which was attended by William Ayers and Obama was one of the presenters who fondly reminisced about the many dinners he shared at the home of Rashid Khalidi and how their conversations "challenged his thinking." While Obama refrained from joining disparaging anti-Israel remarks at the event, his presence at such affairs left some Palestinian American leaders believing that Obama might be more sympathetic to their point of view than he was willing to publicly admit. Even Khalidi himself tolerated Obama's public stance on behalf of Israel because he said he understood that it was a requirement if Obama wanted to win a national election.

In February 2007, Obama announced his candidacy for President of the United States. He broke fundraising records, even garnering more contributions than his nearest rival, Senator Hillary Clinton. Hannity's investigation revealed contributions from groups with terrorist connections such as Hamas and as the race progressed several scandals plagued Obama. Jeremiah Wright, pastor of the church he attended for two decades, was exposed for his racially and politically damning sermons of both white people and America. Wright's Marxist theology was so damaging to Obama's future that Obama subsequently resigned from the church and distanced himself from the pastor.

The Chicago Sun-Times revealed a close relationship between Obama and Syrian-born Tony Rezko,[5] one of Obama's earliest political fund-raisers who was indicted and subsequently convicted on federal corruption charges. Rezko hosted a 2003 cocktail party at his mansion in support of Obama's U.S. senatorial campaign and was part of Obama's senatorial finance committee. Federal indictment documents against Rezko revealed Obama received contributions from Rezko's illegal schemes, which Obama subsequently donated to charity. The law firm that employed Obama did work for Rezko's low-income housing projects and many of Rezko's buildings were located within Obama's state senatorial district. Astonishingly, during the time Rezko was known to be under investigation Obama entered into a questionable 2005 real estate transaction with Rezko's wife. More and more, his Chicago associations raised questions about his ability to judge character or be involved with honorable people.

Mohamed Salim Al-Churbaji served as a fundraiser and organizer of Obama's presidential campaign. His father was a Syrian national who was a member of the Muslim Brotherhood and had close ties to Bassam Ahmad, who fought for Osama Bin Laden.

On July 12, 2007, Obama told the NAACP Presidential Primary Forum that as president he planed to issue an Executive Order repealing gun protection on the grounds the Second Amendment *"is not currently what the Founders intended it to be and only the Army is a militia…not private citizens."*

To freedom loving Americans, a few 'red flags' of concern popped up regarding Obama's apparent lack of sincere patriotism. During a summer event in Iowa, a Time magazine photographer took a picture of Obama, Hillary Clinton, and Bill Richardson during the Pledge of Allegiance. Both Clinton and Richardson had their hands over their hearts. Obama did not. Associated Press journalist Nedra Pickler revealed in her February 23, 2008 column that Obama refused to wear an American flag lapel pin and gave the lame defense that, to him, the pin, *"has become a substitute for real patriotism,"* so he didn't wear it. Michelle Obama tellingly told a Milwaukee audience the she was proud of America, "for the *first time* in my adult life," which caused Cindy McCain to retort that she has *always* been proud of her country.

After one of the most nail biting primaries in history, Obama passed the threshold to become the Democratic presumptive nominee on June 3, 2008. Hillary Clinton suspended her campaign and endorsed him four days later. On August 23, 2008 Senator Joe Biden was chosen to be Obama's vice-presidential running mate and on August 28th, Obama officially accepted the nomination for president at the Denver Democratic National Convention.

While Obama's campaign buzz word was 'change,' Ryan Lizza of the *The New Yorker* pointed out in his July 2008 feature article that Obama's campaign was run on reforming a broken political process, yet *"he has always played politics by the rules as they exist, not as he would like them to exist,"* making his mantra for "change" ring hollow. Additionally, Joe Biden epitomized "politics as usual" with his 20-year entrenchment on The Hill. Little of procedural change was likely given Obama's choice of vice-president.

The newly elected 44th President demonstrated contempt for the Constitution in a 2001 interview on Chicago Public Radio station WBEZ when he disparaged the Constitution as being merely "*a charter of negative liberties*" that tells people what the state and federal government "*can't do to you.*" He went on to deride the U.S. Supreme Court for failing to deal with issues of "*redistribution of wealth*" and if that wasn't enough, he condemned the U.S. Supreme Court for not "<u>breaking free</u> *from the essential constraints that were placed by the Founding Fathers and the Constitution.*" Disturbing words from a man who took a vow to "*uphold the Constitution.*" If he values it so little, what does that say about his intent for the nation?

Voters got a rare glimpse into the *real* Obama when he expressed disdain for the people of Pennsylvania by describing them as, "*clinging to their guns and religion.*" An even more disturbing side of him emerged when Obama created a firestorm of controversy as he was filmed talking to "Joe the Plumber,"[6] about taxes. "Joe" was actually Joe Wurzelbacher of Toledo, Ohio and he became visibly outraged when Obama expressed the Socialist concept of taxing anyone that made more than $250,000 (reduced later to an astounding low of $32,000) so those proceeds could be spent on the poor in an effort to "*spread the wealth around.*" That Socialist comment spread like wildfire and Bill O'Reilly, host of *The No Spin Zone* on Fox News even outright labeled Obama a "Communist" when he appeared as a guest on *The View* TV show in October 2008. Subsequently, "Joe the Plumber" became a focal point of the last presidential debate in October 2008 and a symbol of the 'average' American both candidates claimed they wanted most to help as president. Joe's encounter with Obama also showcased the drastically dissimilar stands between the candidates and provided a seldom seen spontaneous view into the *real* Obama and the unspecified avenue of 'change' he intends to inflict on America.

Regardless of all the proof, Americans continued to view Obama through rose colored glasses and the liberal media persistently painted him with a rock star status and his campaign continued to climb the charts.

Obama invoked emotionally charged phrases and the hypnotic style of Adolph Hitler to mesmerize listeners. Senator John McCain angrily claimed Obama would *"say anything to get elected"* and it appeared he was right because Obama flipflopped on numerous issues depending on who he was addressing and he seemed to have an intuitive sense about what voters needs were and promised them whatever they wanted to hear. Like a Pied Piper, voters continued to ignore the facts to follow and support him even though Obama had never defined precisely what *his* version of 'change' would look like.

Obama supporters tended to be the uninformed or liberal left who fell under his charismatic spell and felt it was 'cool' to support a candidate based solely on race or to blindly follow a candidate who was less than honest about his life and intended accomplishments as president. The resulting damage was something Obama didn't want voters to know about…at least not until he was safely in the Oval Office…and then, of course, it would be too late.

The great mystery is *why* otherwise sensible people lost all logic and perspective when Obama's links to unsavory characters and even radical terrorists who intended great harm to America were proven and when his own rhetoric often exposed his Socialist leanings. People simply ignored the warning signs to vote for him anyway. If the past history of his actions and associations prove correct, Obama demonstrated he would say or do anything to get elected but would then have to figure out how he could repay those to whom he sold his soul and to whom he owed endless 'pay-backs' as a result of his journey into history. The prolific trail of evidence would seem to point to the fact we very well may witness the "final chapter" with Obama's administration.

JOSEPH BIDEN, JR.

Joseph Biden, Jr. was elected a U.S. Senator from Delaware in 1972, which makes him the longest serving of the current senators. His election made him the nation's first Roman Catholic vice-president and the first vice-president from Delaware.

He grew up in East coast middle class where his father worked as a car salesman. While attending college he received five student draft deferments and was eventually reclassified by the Selective Service as "not available for service" due to his childhood asthma. He played no part in the anti-war movement that was going on during that time.

In 1966 he married for the first time and had two sons and one daughter. He was elected to the U.S. Senate in 1972 but before he could take the oath of office his wife and daughter were killed in an auto accident. His sons were seriously injured and Biden wound up taking the oath of office from his son's hospital bedside. An instant single father, Biden began a 90-minute commute by Amtrak every day to Washington, D.C. and another 90-minute trip back home each night so he would be there for his sons.

After five years as a single father, Biden remarried in 1977 and had a daughter. His elder son Beau became Delaware's Attorney General and then went to Iraq in 2008 with the Delaware Army National Guard to serve as a JAG – Judge Advocate General. His younger son Hunter is an attorney in Washington, D.C. and sits on the board of directors for Amtrak.

Rated an above average lifetime liberal, Biden served on many key committees during his years in the Senate, among them the prestigious Foreign Relations Committee.

Biden is listed as one of the least wealthy members of the senate, a designation he should be proud of since it demonstrates his honesty in the face of tremendous special interest temptation.

The 2008 presidential race was not Biden's first campaign for president. He also ran in 1988 but withdrew early from both races due to poor showings in the polls. In August 2008 Barack

Obama announced he had chosen Biden as his vice presidential running mate because he felt Biden had the foreign policy and national security experience needed for the times as well as an appeal to the middle class and a willingness to aggressively challenge John McCain. While known as a strong speaker, many wondered if Biden's tendency to blurt out off-putting comments and his long time entrenchment in Washington's politics-as-usual atmosphere might be a detriment to the campaign. He seemed an unlikely choice for the message of "change" that Obama wished to portray.

On October 2, 2008 Biden and Alaska Governor Sarah Palin who was John McCain's choice for vice-president, met for their only vice-presidential debate. Feisty and down-to-earth Palin exceeded all expectations and left Biden in the dust. The strong speaker met his match.

JOHN McCAIN III

John McCain III entered the race for president with two major factors against him; he was snookered into signing a campaign contribution restriction pledge and the media was hugely biased in favor of his opponent.

The 2008 presidential campaign proved to be one of the most biased, deceitful, and acrimonious political campaigns in history and the national media made sure Barack Obama was given a free ride while presenting John McCain with a mountain to climb. McCain established himself as a man of integrity who placed country above his own personal desires yet the media continued to disregard a laundry list of scandals and questionable associations connected to his opponent and the public displayed total blind indifference to 'red flags' that should have given them great pause

John McCain took pride in being labeled a "maverick" because, in his view, that meant he fought "politics as usual" and he and his equally "maverick" vice presidential choice, Alaska Governor Sarah Palin, intended their main focus as America's leaders to be "cleaning house" in Washington, D.C.

It is not surprising then that McCain had been a "maverick" his entire life. Born into a military family, both his grandfather and father were four-star Navy admirals with outstanding careers in the armed forces. After graduating from high school in 1954 McCain continued the family tradition by attending the U.S. Naval Academy in Annapolis where he was more interested in standing up for those who were being bullied than in studying. His penchant for paying little attention to the rules caused him to place close to last in class ranking but his priority was fairness for his classmates so little effort was put into improving his class standing. Regardless, he graduated in 1958.

McCain married a model named Carol Shepp in 1965 and adopted her young son and daughter.

After he became a naval pilot he crashed twice and even hit power lines on another occasion. Nevertheless, he was assigned to the aircraft carrier *USS Forrestal* after requesting combat assignment, where he flew A-4 Skyhawks during the Vietnam War. It was during this time that he was nearly killed. His burning jet was near the center of the July 29, 1967 *Forrestal* fire and a bomb went off while he was trying to help another pilot escape. The ensuing fire took 24-hours to control and cost 134 sailors their lives. McCain was injured but asked for reassignment to the *USS Oriskany* due to the *Forrestal* being out of commission.

Only three months later McCain was flying his 23rd bombing mission over North Vietnam when a missle shot him down over Hanoi. Seriously injured, he became a prisoner of war in the infamous 'Hanoi Hilton.' Medical care was finally given to him only after discovering McCain's father was a top admiral but he remained in solitary confinement for two years and his torture continued.

McCain's father was named commander of all U.S. forces in Vietnam in 1968 so McCain was offered early release as a propaganda effort by the VC to be seen as 'compassionate.' McCain refused the offer unless every prisoner taken captive before him was released as well. Loyalty to his men not only resulted in a refusal by the VC to honor his request but intensified his torture as well. His injuries over the remaining five and a half years as a POW left him with permanent disabilities and even a suicide attempt when he reached the end of what he could endure as a POW. He has stated that being a POW taught him that he was *"no longer my own man, but my country's."* He was released from captivity in March 1973 but the bravery and character he displayed during that dark time forever changed him and forged his fiercely patriotic commitment to put "country first."

After returning to the United States McCain spent a significant amount of time undergoing treatment for his injuries, which he knew would prevent him from being promoted to a full admiral like his father and grandfather. Instead, he got his flight status reinstated and became the commanding officer of a Florida training squadron.

In 1977 McCain served as the Navy's liaison to the U.S. Senate gaining congressional financing for a new supercarrier the Carter administration opposed. It also ignited a passion for public service and his future second career.

He became a prisoner of war only two years into his marriage to Carol and in 1969 Carol was injured in a car accident. Both husband and wife faced their own struggles with rehabilitation and figuring out where their marriage was to go after not seeing each other for nearly six years. He admits he had extramarital affairs during his assignment in Florida, which caused his marriage to Carol to deteriorate. Time, circumstance, and McCain's roving eye took its toll. By the time he met Cindy Lou Hensley in 1979 his marriage to Carol was essentially over. McCain fell hard for the Phoenix teacher and asked Carol for a divorce, which she granted. It was uncontested and McCain made sure Carol received the houses and financial support for her medical treatments. He remained involved in his adopted son and daughter's lives and Carol and John maintained a friendly relationship.

Cindy Hensley and John McCain were married in 1980 and because she was wealthy due to her father's substantial beer distributorship, they signed a prenuptial agreement to keep her family's assets under her name alone and have always maintained separate finances and income tax returns.

Shortly after the marriage McCain retired from the Navy and went to work as a public relations vice president for his father-in-law's Anheuser-Busch beer distributorship. It put him in contact with powerful people and eventually McCain used those contacts as a base for his 1982 campaign for Arizona's open seat for Congress. He found he was always fighting the label of "carpetbagger" and would become famous for his response to yet another reporter's taunt regarding his newcomer status. He replied that his family was a military family so they moved often and didn't have the luxury of staying in one place like so many non-military families and – when he thought about it – the place he actually lived the longest in his life was – Hanoi. The insults stopped and he won the election.

When icon U.S. Senator Barry Goldwater retired, McCain ran for his seat and became Arizona's U.S. Senator in 1987. He sat on important committees such as the Armed Services Committee, Indian Affairs Committee, and Commerce Committee and delivered a speech at the 1988 Republican National Convention, which escalated public awareness of his political potential. In his infamous "maverick" manner he battled establishment perspectives, helped normalize diplomatic relations with Vietnam in 1995, and objected to 'pork barrel' spending. He was most proud of the 2002 passage of the Bipartisan Campaign Reform Act aka the McCain-Feingold bill[7] to limit corrupting special interest "soft money" influence.

Paradoxically, McCain was named in the "Keating Five" scandal[8] in the late 1980s. While doing PR work for his father-in-law, one of the powerful figures he met was banker Charles Keating, Jr. who contributed $112,000 in lawful contributions from himself and his associates at the Lincoln Savings and Loan Association over a period of time during McCain's senatorial tenures. When Keating found himself embroiled in a regulatory investigation crisis McCain was one of five senators he contacted to intervene on his behalf with government officials to prevent the seizure of Lincoln Savings and Loan. McCain met twice with federal regulators to discuss the matter, which resulted in all five senators having to appear before the Senate Ethics Committee charged with improper intervention or violating Senate rules. Keating received a five year prison sentence for corrupt mismanagement but it was determined that McCain's role in the scandal was minor and he was cleared of all charges. McCain acknowledged his actions conveyed the wrong impression of undue influence, was the wrong thing to do, and he had exercised poor judgment but the committee determined he acted in good faith, if not good judgment, in responding to the needs of a constituent. Despite his lapse of common sense, McCain easily won re-election in 1992.

He published his memoir *Faith of My Fathers* in 1999, which became a bestseller about McCain's family, childhood, and service during the Vietnam War, including his years as a

POW. It was made into a film that movingly demonstrated the strength and character of this remarkable man.

The same year McCain announced his candidacy for president but was shuffled aside by the Republican Party who had anointed Texas Governor George W. Bush. McCain became the target of political brutality when Bush and special interest groups McCain had challenged in the past pulled out painfully cruel stops in order to ensure that Bush would win. While in the presence of Bush, McCain was accused by a veterans activist of abandoning veterans and Bush made no effort to dispute that lie. The smear campaign against McCain included lies that he had an affair that resulted in the dark skinned child Cindy had actually brought home from a Mother Teresa run Bangladesh orphanage, that McCain was a homosexual, Cindy was a drug addict, and that McCain was 'unbalanced' from his days as a POW. The vicious rumors, Bush's ability to outspend McCain, and Bush's mobilizing of evangelical voters left McCain in a "very dark place" and his campaign never recovered. He withdrew from the race in March 2000.

Bitter antagonism remained between Bush and McCain but after the events of September 11, 2001 McCain put those feelings aside to support the president and the U.S. attack on Afghanistan. He and Senator Joe Lieberman created the 9/11 Commission bill. Seven years after first presenting the McCain-Feingold campaign finance bill, it finally passed both houses in 2002, which McCain saw as his greatest legislative accomplishment.

McCain introduced the McCain Detainee Amendment to the Defense Appropriations bill for 2005, which prohibited inhumane treatment of prisoners and strongly supported the 2007 Iraq troop surge. In April 2007 he announced his intention to again run for President of the United States.

He ran against a formidable field of candidates and was largely seen as the underdog who suffered from campaign staff problems, low fundraising, and bad poll numbers and was given next to no chance of emerging as the Republican nominee. He rode his bus, the 'Straight Talk Express,' to an infinite number of events, took part in debates and free media events, garnered the endorsement of numerous newspapers, picked up Independent supporters, and won the New Hampshire primary. He went on to win in other states and ultimately won both the majority of states and delegates in the Super Tuesday Republican primary to become the presumptive Republican nominee.

His opponent in the general election was Barack Obama and that election cycle started off in a dishonorable manner. McCain and Obama both agreed to sign a pledge that they would "cap" their campaign spending at $84-million each and forego matching federal funds. McCain signed the pledge but Obama reneged at the last minute. The broken promise by Obama meant he had access to unlimited funds while McCain signed in good faith but was left to be vastly – and unfairly - outspent.

Tremendous media bias helped sway voters with CNN as the worst offender. For every negative stated about Obama, seven were cited against McCain. Regardless of the scandals and criminal associations surrounding Obama, the public turned a blind eye, goaded on by the left-wing liberal media.

While Obama chose Washington, D.C. entrenched Joe Biden as his vice presidential running mate, McCain shocked America by introducing Alaska Governor Sarah Palin to be his partner. She was a breath of fresh air and came with "maverick" credentials of her own. Like McCain, Palin "took on" established politicians even in her own party and battled the big oil companies and won. She was an immensely popular governor who was very successful in running her state. As dedicated as McCain to "cleaning house" in Washington if they were elected, Palin drew record crowds everywhere she went and connected with audiences because they recognized she truly was "one of them." Palin was a clear shot in the arm for the McCain campaign and an articulate defender of McCain's conservative values.

Some voters were concerned with McCain's age since he would have been 72 if inaugurated in 2009 but life is uncertain and there is no assurance that radicals wouldn't end

Obama's life with a bullet or that he might develop a fatal illness or become the victim of an unforeseen accident. To base the choice of a president on age rather than which is best suited for the country, was foolish. McCain was a moderate conservative who often reached across the aisle for bi-partisan cooperation, support, and results. His strong personal character exuded integrity and honor and his military service and years as a POW cemented his love for America and his dedication to putting his country first. He maintained close family ties to all his children from both marriages and his maverick persona made him popular with voters who were disillusioned with endless politics-as-usual. He was an honest man who valued 'straight talk' and admitted his shortcomings and even apologized for them. He was the first to poke fun at himself and exhibit his sense of humor. Above all else, Senator John McCain was a man who would do whatever it took to make sure America and her citizens were in good hands. During a dark time when the country was divided over so many issues, the economy was failing, unemployment was reaching record breaking heights, the future was unsure, and the nation was experiencing unrest, instability, and fear…John McCain provided Americans with the most important gift of all…hope.

SARAH PALIN

Sarah Palin hit the national political scene like a hurricane closing in on the Gulf coast. Beautiful, bright, articulate, and with a proven record of her own in governing the State of Alaska, her down-to-earth rebel style made her a perfect fit for a McCain/Palin partnership goal of cleaning up government corruption. Wherever she appeared her exceptional ability to speak spontaneously and energize any crowd she addressed was simply amazing to watch. The remarkable thing about America is that it always seems to uncover ordinary people who do extraordinary things. Sarah was everything good America stood for and she was a natural and authentic Patriot. Anyone listening to her knew they not only could believe what she was saying but that she and John McCain would make good on their promise to return accountability, responsibility, and honor to government. Even more important, at a time when a collective nation felt only despair for the future, Sarah Palin radiated hope.

A passionate advocate of her state, McCain first recognized her authentic personality, love for her country, and maverick persona at the National Governors Association meeting in Washington in Febrary 2008. Instantly impressed, he invited her to meet with him at his home in Arizona in August 2008. She was the only potential vice presidential contender to meet with McCain in person because during that visit he was so certain she was the right person as a partner for his ticket that he offered her the position.

His assessment was accurate but the vicious liberal media instantly made her the focus of a disgraceful character assassination and insult crusade. She endured much, much more than any man would have been subjected to had he been in her place. Despite petty scrutiny, downright lies, and hurtful personal attacks, Sarah held her head high and continued to fight for what she knew was more important than the actions of narrow minded malicious liberals who feared her popularity and ability to energize the nation.

After obtaining her Bachelor of Science degree in communications-journalism from the University of Idaho in 1987, she worked as a sports reporter for both Anchorage TV stations and a local newspaper. In 1992 she won a seat on the Wasilla city council where she made certain the city sales tax was spent wisely. Although she was reelected in 1995, she only served one year of that term because she ran for mayor in 1996, defeating a three-term incumbent mayor. She continued to target wasteful spending by consolidating agencies and even cutting her own salary by 10%. She significantly cut property taxes due to a 2% sales tax that existed prior to her election as mayor. Municipal bonds allowed improvements to the roads and sewers and she gave additional funding to the police department. Palin's main focus in her political career was reform and she employed action to back up her words.

When term limits prevented a third term as mayor she ran for lieutenant governor placing second in the primary.

The governor appointed her to the Alaska Oil and Gas Conservation Commission serving as the Ethics Supervisor. She claimed a "lack of ethics" within her fellow Republicans on the commission and resigned in 2004. Palin then filed a formal ethics complaint against the Alaska Republican Party Chair which accused him of doing work for the party on public time since he also was an Oil and Gas Conservation Commissioner so she felt he was working closely with a company he was supposed to regulate as well. She also filed a conflict of interest ethics complaint against a former Alaska Attorney General. Both subjects resigned and the oil company executive paid a significant fine. Palin clearly demonstrated her intention to rid government of corruption even if it meant taking on those in her own party. Her reputation as a reformer was solidly established.

She became Alaska's first female governor when she defeated a former governor despite the fact he outspent her. She was the first governor to have been born after Alaska became a state and the youngest governor in the state's history. Her focus was to clean up corruption in Alaska politics and to push ethics reform. She showed her word was her honor when she made good on her campaign promise to sell the governor's jet. She supported a decreased dependence on federal funds and cut back on 'pork-barrel' projects. Under her watchful eye state revenues doubled even though Alaska enjoys no sales tax or personal income tax. The most important accomplishment of her term, however, was the bill she signed in August 2008 awarding a license to build and operate a pipeline from the North Slope through Canada to the continental U.S. to transport natural gas.

Palin has shown herself to be a very capable leader who was strong enough to make the decisions that were not always popular but were best for the people of Alaska. She never hesitated to battle unethical bureaucrats even if they were members of her own party. She always made decisions in the best interest of Alaska's citizens and she was hugely popular.

Palin was the whole package and that created a firestorm of fear and envy from liberals after Sen. John McCain picked her to be his running mate. She was subjected to unwarranted innuendos, outright lies, and cruel personal attacks that would not have happened had she been male.

She was criticized for accepting a legally entitled travel per diem between her office in the capital at Juneau and her home office of Anchorage despite the fact she waived reimbursement for lodging and chose to drive the hour to her home in Wasilla rather than stay in Anchorage at taxpayer's expense. Additionally, she declined to use the former governor's private chef. State expenses attested to the fact that Palin's gubernatorial expenses were 80% below those of her predecessor but the Democrats and the media wouldn't give her any credit.

She was also criticized for expenses related to bringing her family to selected political invitations for which their attendance was expected. Under that condition their attendance was designated as "state business" and therefore a legally permitted expense.

She endured ridicule and hateful personal attacks on a regular basis including unkind and even marginally libelous skits on *Saturday Night Live* by Tina Fey whose impersonations were often disrespectful and mean spirited. Nevertheless, Palin appeared on the program to poke fun at herself and showcase that, in the end, she was a regular person with a great sense of humor who could "take the heat." Her appearance not only portrayed a very human side of an authentic person, it also resulted in the highest rating SNL had received in 14 years.

The nastiest attack was nicknamed "troopergate"[9] and involved the firing of the Public Safety Commissioner who claimed his dismissal was in great part tied in with pressure to get rid of a state trooper who was embroiled in an acrimonious custody battle regarding his divorce from Palin's sister. Palin fired the commissioner for performance related issues but the commissioner claimed he had received undue pressure to fire Palin's brother-in-law and he felt the real reason for his dismissal was because he refused to do her bidding. The trooper allegedly used a tazer on his 11-year old stepson to "show him how it feels and to prove he wasn't a mommy's boy," made a death threat against his father-in-law, drank on the job, used steroids, and shot a moose without a permit. An internal investigation by law enforcement upheld some of the charges but dismissed others and gave the trooper a suspension for misconduct citing a "serious and unacceptable pattern of activity over a lengthy period of time," but did not fire him because he was protected by his police union. The Alaska legislature hired an investigator to evaluate the circumstances and two months later the report was released and determined the governor had a "proper and lawful" right to fire the commissioner under her "constitutional and statutory authority." While the report felt there very well may have been a personal agenda involved in pressure to fire the trooper, Palin was found to have had the authority to fire the commissioner. A second investigation by the Alaska Personnel Board demanded both Todd and Sarah Palin submit to depositions that could have resulted in criminal penalties but in the end they cleared her of any ethical misconduct. While state agencies wrangled over jurisdiction in the complicated matter, misrepresentation, outright lies, and exaggerations were the order of the day by Democrats and the liberal media in an effort to hurt Palin and derail her campaign with negative coverage.

The most vicious lies, however, were lobbed at Palin's family. They included accusations of affairs, that the new baby actually belonged to the governor's daughter, that Todd Palin had molested his daughters, and an entire condemnation of her daughter's pregnancy. Nothing appeared to be off-limits with the vicious attacks yet if anything negative was said about Obama the race card was instantly pulled out and the comment in question was declared 'racist.' There has never been an uglier or more one-sided campaign in America's history.

In reality, Palin married her childhood sweetheart Todd Palin and they had five children. Their oldest son Track enlisted in the U.S. Army six years to the day of the tragic 9/11 attack and his infantry brigade was deployed to Iraq in September 2008 for a year-long maneuver. Palin's oldest daughter Bristol became pregnant by her long time boyfriend Levi Johnston who appeared on the campaign trail with Palin's family. Bristol and Levi planned to wed and raise the baby together but the family received scathing abuse from liberals amid accusations that Palin's "family values" fell short for a vice presidential candidate. Trig was a Downs Syndrome baby that opened dialogue for parents all over the nation with special needs children because Palin pledged to be an advocate for them in her capacity as vice president. Todd was employed as an oil field production operator as well as owning his own commercial fishing business and was a gifted athlete who competed in the rugged Iron Dog snowmachine race – even once finishing the 2000 mile race with a broken arm but protected from further injury by the required helmet and body armor.

During her speech at the Republican National Convention in St. Paul, Minnesota in September 2008, Palin quipped, "*Some people use change to promote their career while others use their career to promote change.*" She was ready to fight back and she took on Obama with a steel spine and a smile and raised questions about the problematic and even Socialist sounding direction his 'change' would take the nation.

None of the three men in the race for the top two jobs in the land had ever run an entire state or been commander-in-chief of the state's armed forces yet the media continued to disrespect and discount Palin's abilities and experience and nearly salivated at the thought of seeing her fail in the only vice presidential debate. Palin not only was extremely knowledgeable and articulate about every subject during the October 2, 2008 debate but viewers could actually see Democrat Joe Biden slowly wither into a sedate shell as Palin ran circles around him. The woman the media continued to bash as not being prepared to be president simply left Biden in the dust and exceeded most voters' expectations.

The uptight strait-laced East coast ivy league section of the country simply did not understand this gracious unaffected no-nonsense woman who minced no words and meant what she said in a down home spontaneous but extremely savvy and articulate manner. Palin was a conservative with a strong sense of right and wrong and a desire to remove any "good ole boy" network from government and return it to the people as the nation's Founders intended. She was a lifelong member of NRA, supported capital punishment, opposed same-sex marriage, was pro-life, advocated sex education in public schools, did not champion stem cell research, believed global warming was partly natural and partly caused by man's activities, promoted oil and natural gas resource exploration in Alaska, supported preemptive military action if imminent threat existed, and supported NATO membership for the Ukraine and Georgia as well as protecting them in the face of a Russian invasion if they became NATO members.

Sarah Palin proved herself to be the excellent choice John McCain knew her to be but the most disturbing element of the 2008 presidential campaign was the over-the-edge vicious attacks by liberals who left no insult or lie unturned over petty issues like the GOP paying for Palin's vice presidential campaign wardrobe, which was to be auctioned off for charity after the election but when the Republicans fought back against a Socialist leftwing tactic, no criticism regarding Barack Obama was tolerated. Criminal association and Socialist policies were off limits despite the fact the nation's voters had every right to an open and transparent discussion about who and what Obama was since he was seeking the highest office in the land and what he did as president would certainly affect every American.

At the end of the day, Sarah Palin is an exceptional woman and a dedicated Patriot who may very well become the nation's first female president by running on her own merits one day. One fact is very clear….she is one-of-a-kind and she definitely energized the 2008 election.

Chapter 22

AMERICA'S FUTURE

On November 4, 2008 history was made. America voted in record numbers and in the end, half the nation was jubilant while half was disheartened. By a popular vote of 52% to 46%, Americans elected Barack Hussein Obama their 44th president, the first black president in the nation's history. He is also the first Democrat since Jimmy Carter to receive more than half the popular vote and the first senator to be elected president since John F. Kennedy. Martin Luther King, Jr. could never have imagined when he uttered his infamous words, *"We shall overcome,"* that a result of the civil rights movement would eventually culminate in the election of a black man to the highest office in the land.

Voters had an ax to grind at the polls. Many voters were so angry at the Bush administration that they lodged their protest by voting Democrat. Not only did Bush leave the nation fighting two wars but the national economy had declined into a massive recession, unemployment skyrocketed, and citizens were much worse off than they were before the 43rd president took office. Had George W. Bush not been president when the 2008 election occurred, it is quite possible considering the close popular vote that John McCain might very well have won the election. If one thing cost John McCain the election, it was George W. Bush.

Additionally, McCain failed to demonstrate strong leadership during the Wall Street melt down, admitted the economy was not his strong suit despite the fact that issue was the most important one to voters, never recovered from his perceived association with George W. Bush, and refused to aggressively challenge Obama's questionable association with terrorists until it was too late.

Perhaps McCain's fate was sealed long ago when President Ronald Reagan set forth an "11th Commandment," which he proclaimed as, *"Thou shalt not criticize a fellow Republican."* That dim-witted dribble contributed to reluctance on the part of the GOP to 'police' their own in weeding out officials that were not ethical, honorable, or viable. Democrats recognized that and used it to their advantage with the result being a huge rift within the Republican Party itself that gave Democrats a winning advantage. A myriad of things played into the demise of McCain's dream for America and Obama's dramatic victory and experts such as media consultant Mark McKinnon aptly observed that, *"It may have turned out that no Republican could have won."*

The biggest culprit in creating a biased election was the media – in particular, CNN-TV who went out of their way to suppress any criticism or negative fact about Obama yet hammered Sarah Palin relentlessly. Ted Turner is an ultra-liberal and founder of cable-TV network CNN. His influence as well as the broadcasting giant's financial ties to the Middle East certainly shed light as to why CNN constantly bulldozed the campaign of John McCain and especially why it massacred the qualifications and reputation of McCain's running mate Alaska Governor Sarah Palin while doing everything they could to avoid talking about Obama's past disreputable associations and Socialist views. Late in the general election, McCain finally fought back and was branded a "nasty and negative" campaigner because he stood up for himself. Every time McCain's campaign brought up a relevant fact about Obama's questionable associations or activities, the Obama campaign pulled out the 'race card' to effectively silence any criticism. The 2008 election *was* about race because the race card was used to intimidate those who tried to bring out negative facts. Even broadcasting jobs were put in jeopardy if certain negative information about Obama was not suppressed. If anyone 'elected' Obama, it was the biased media who fueled an ugly race with their liberal invectives and CNN was the biggest culprit in promoting that biased coverage. It was so deliberate that even the other major networks took CNN to task for it. In the end, the race boiled down to one truly history changing fact: one candidate was basically an unknown with questionable intent for the country and the other was well tested and known and put his country above himself. Despite not knowing who Barack Obama *really* was, half the nation elevated him to the Office of the President.

While other candidates followed the accepted protocol of the dutiful spouse and family standing behind them on stage in a show of support, Obama regularly bounced up the steps alone commanding center stage – and singular attention. Oprah Winfrey christened Obama "The One" while radical Nation of Islam leader Louis Farrakhan dubbed him "The Messiah" and his ego lives up to it. That confidence motivated him to climb the ladder in whatever manner necessary including associating with radicals to gain the monetary and networking contacts needed to attain the office he desired.

Obama's meteoric rise from serving only one-half of his only term as U.S. Senator from Illinois to President of the United States was simply stunning. Voters were disgruntled with eight years of the Bush administration's follies and desperately desired a change that would improve their lives. That propelled Obama to victory but he was in the public eye so short a time before becoming elected that voters hardly had the time to evaluate who the man was that could mesmerize millions with his rock star quality performances and was able to command enormous campaign contributions never before seen by candidates' coffers. The nation was riveted by the smooth talking charismatic young man throughout the primary election despite the fact disturbing associations and discoveries began to surface and he never explained what HIS view of 'change' looked like. Only during the general election did a substantial amount of alarming information about the candidate become widely known and that was hardly enough time for a nation to sort out the facts and make an informed decision about a person who would impact citizens' lives and take America down an unknown path.

The voting public was almost equally divided into two camps: those who saw Barack Obama as someone who would 'save' them and 'change' their lives for the better and those who had genuine concerns about a man who remained largely an unknown mystery. The latter category worried that Obama simply wasn't qualified to be president. His brief stints in elected office were limited only to that of Illinois state senator and one unfinished term as a U.S. senator; hardly enough experience to be elevated to the highest office in the land. Unlike Sarah Palin, his opponent's vice presidential running mate, Obama had not even been the top executive of a state nor carried out the responsibilities for running it, nor had he ever been commander-in-chief of a state's armed forces. He simply did not possess the experience needed to run a nation, yet voters were so entranced with him that they were willing to cast a blind vote for someone about whom the nation knew almost nothing.

Occasionally a person exhibits two totally different personalities. In public Obama was a charismatic and hypnotic novelty but privately he showed traits of deceit and betrayal. Disquietingly however, is the fact one doesn't cancel out the other.

Obama has been surrounded by a cloud of suspicion from the moment his questionable Chicago associations became public but most disturbing is the question of his eligibility to be president and specifically, his steadfast refusal to provide documentation to prove where he was born. If there is even the slightest question regarding a candidate's place of birth it is incumbent upon the U.S. Supreme Court to hear this most basic of constitutional appeals. An issue of this great magnitude cannot go unanswered as no other court case will ever be more important than determining if the man elected to the highest office in the land is indeed eligible as the U.S. Constitution outlines.

Some may argue that John McCain was not born in America so why should anyone care about Obama's place of birth. There is a distinct difference, however. McCain was born at the Coco Solo Naval Air Station in Panama, which was under U.S. control at the time. Not only were both his parents

American citizens, he came from a military family and his father was stationed in Panama at the time. Anyone born on foreign soil of American parents who are stationed there due to the military, is automatically an indisputable American citizen. That differs greatly from Obama's unclear situation.

Obama constantly promised "transparency" in his administration during his campaign yet issue after issue, the public is met with a stubborn lack of disclosure. If he had nothing to hide he himself should have made the document available since the issue is at the heart of the Constitution's edicts but he has not done that. Until that is done the nation will always feel it may have been tricked into electing a man who was not a 'natural born' citizen and will continue to wonder if Obama lied to get elected and if the Supreme Court was duplicite in covering up that illegal fraudulent action. It is a deceptive way to begin a presidency and integrity of both the presidency and the Supreme Court can only remain under a cloud of distrust and suspicion by its citizens as a result.

Even Obama's longstanding association with terrorists and criminals and his unwillingness to divulge personal background information, medical test results, college transcripts, or even his senior thesis failed to stop the mad rush to the polls to pull a lever for a man with many unanswered questions and a mysterious unknown intent for America's future. Associations with people like socialist Saul Alinsky, terrorist William Ayers, and radical Rashid Khalidi gave pause to many voters. Once factual information began surfacing about Obama's questionable alliances with radicals, a cloud of misgiving followed the remainder of his campaign days but those who wanted to believe he could perform miracles chose to turn a blind eye and vote for him anyway.

One such alliance was radical Rashid Kahalidi. In a tape of a farewell party thrown for his 'friend' Khalidi, most of those attending could be heard to condemn Israel yet Obama remained silent and then went on to appoint an Orthodox Jew as his chief of staff after the election. That seemed to substantiate the fact he may have associated with radicals but may not necessarily have embraced their extreme views.

Radio interviews such as the one in 2001 on WBEZ in Los Angeles where Obama himself spewed socialist rhetoric about the "negative Constitution" and the failure of America to "spread the wealth" created fear for voters who cared more about a candidate's loyalty to America and electing a qualified contender who sincerely placed the nation's welfare above their own. Unfortunately Obama is basically an unknown entity so it is uncertain whether he will take a traditional or ominous avenue in his position as president.

Both Obama and McCain pledged to sign an agreement to reject taxpayer funds for their campaigns but Obama reneged at the last minute, which left him free to pull in huge contributions while holding McCain to the much more restricted perimeters of the campaign finance limits. Obama's ensuing unparalleled fund-raising ability contributed in large part to his success in winning the presidency because it gave him the ability to 'buy' exposure and other endeavors not available to lesser-funded opponents. By election day Obama had raised nearly one-billion dollars, a sum unheard of in any prior presidential race. He pulled in huge contributions from a lucrative Internet donor drive as well as colossal donations from major organizations, their members, families, and employees. Even Obama's old alma maters, Columbia and Harvard Universities, contributed nearly one-million each. Obama's cloudy FEC campaign contribution report does not list many who donated, especially those who gave through his Internet site. In that vein, two individuals deemed to have violated FEC rules are Monir and Hosam Edwan, residents of the Rafah area, a large refugee camp in the Gaza Strip that is controlled by Hamas. They admit to contributing more than $29,500 to Obama's on-line campaign. FEC rules prohibit foreigners from donating and one person cannot contribute more than $2300 in a single campaign. In the end, the identity of many contributors remained unknown and questions regarding Obama's campaign finances remained unanswered.

An organization that became a thorn in Obama's side during his campaign was ACORN (Association of Community Organizations for Reform Now), which is an organization that has a long history of corrupting the political process with questionable election activities and fraud and has been investigated in at least a dozen states. It is a shrewd family owned business headquartered in Louisiana that evolved into a multi-million-dollar conglomerate. Obama was involved with a Chicago based ACORN training session when he worked as a "community organizer." The company is registered as a non-profit corporation so no public financial disclosure is required and since it operates a virtual self-contained economy, few financial documents are available for public examination. The primary ACORN organization has dozens of "offshoots" and even formed two labor unions, which leads to public confusion about the power structure of the group and how it is actually run. A rare insight was provided in 1987 by former Arkansas ACORN chair Dorothy Perkins who claimed the group was run like a cult under the iron fist of founder Wade Rathke where "*all the money ended up under Wade Rathke's control and was never seen by the low-income individuals the organization claims to represent.*"[1]. Rathke was so controlling that when management was at odds with organizers, the members were the ones who were forced out. That resulted in a 2003 NLRB decision against ACORN management who found them guilty of using union-busting tactics against their own employees. Employees are routinely subjected to problems such as not being paid a fair wage, not being paid overtime, and even being robbed and sexually assaulted while working in unsafe environments. That resulted in violations of the "get out the vote" campaign when workers fraudulently filled out voter registrations in order to meet their 'quota' or face losing their jobs. The FBI raided several national locations of ACORN for which Obama's counsel blamed the Bush White House, hypocritically ignoring the fact the voter registration political arm of ACORN was endorsed by Obama who had worked on behalf of ACORN as an attorney. Additionally, Obama and William Ayers awarded money to ACORN while sitting on the board of the Woods Fund foundation. Voter fraud by ACORN was rampant in the 2008 election yet the issue just seemed to 'disappear' after Obama was elected. Fox-TV felt revealing the extent of ACORN corruption and illegal activity was so important to the issue of free elections that they continued making the public aware of the extent of illegal activity on ACORN's part so the 2010 mid-elections would not be compromised. At this juncture, the fate of this traitorous organization will not be known for some time.

Citizens who researched candidates were leery of Obama's socialist associations and viewpoints and feared he would take America down a government controlled path should he be elected. The nation's economic crisis tends to give credence to that notion when one views the numerous 'bailouts' occurring with banks, financial institutions, a proposal of socialized medicine, the takeover of private pension plans to infuse additional revenue into federal coffers, a potential windfall profit tax on any business that produces a profit, speculation of a bailout for the auto industry, and Obama's now infamous statement that he intends to *"spread the wealth."*

Judicious voters feared a leader with socialist leanings because that system of beliefs could lead to a dictatorship. The Bush administration did absolutely nothing to stem the flow of illegal immigrants into the U.S. from Mexico during the eight years he was in office. The invasion by third world people who know nothing about liberty and freedom but who are more than happy to take American welfare handouts and services are also willing to accept any curtailment on their freedom in exchange for governmental freebies because they come from a culture where they are used to being told what to do. As more and more people from undeveloped countries swarm into the U.S. and become the majority, it would make it easier for a dictatorship to become reality and for freedom loving citizens who oppose the loss of freedom to be conquered.

For voters who were informed and researched the candidates, this was a very real fear given the unknown nature of the Democratic hopeful.

The election gave Congress a Democratic majority as well so for the first time in 15 years, Democrats will control both the White House and Congress. That is a precarious alignment when one considers the necessity for check and balances.

As a politician who was willing to promise anything to get elected, Obama's rhetoric contained endless pledges even he knew he couldn't keep – or never intended to keep. <u>Now he has to deliver</u>.

Obama has inherited daunting obstacles as he enters his presidency so the nation holds its breath as it watches his choices for his Cabinet and top advisors. His inexperience is obvious so he would be prudent to surround himself with the wisest and most cautious minds in politics but his past associations and Socialist influence makes the public uneasy about the people he will choose to be his advisors and enforcers.

Never has the nation been so divided and never has the nation faced such dramatic change in its basic make-up as it has with the election of Barack Obama. Exit polls showed Obama attained victory through the votes of the impressionable young, blacks and minorities, and women. Additionally, the labor unions provided millions of votes for Obama by threatening jobs, intimidating workers, and brainwashing members. Unions routinely support candidates that are pro-union but the 2008 presidential election was unusual in that none of the presidential or vice-presidential candidates had direct ties to labor unions with the exception of Sarah Palin. Her husband Todd was a union steelworker and her intended son-in-law was an electrical union apprentice. Nevertheless, the labor unions supported Obama instead, perhaps due to union bias against women but more likely because Obama co-sponsored a "card check" bill known as The Employee Free Choice Act, which would benefit labor unions. Union members were told to vote Democrat. Their PAC money was decided for them even if they wanted some of it to be spent on the GOP race. They were told their jobs depended on voting Democrat.

Members, including the author's union member husband, were called by the union and asked how they would vote and if they intended to vote Republican they were told they would be placed on "the list," which meant they could be blackballed from employment dispatch calls. The unions deluged members with massive messages telling them how 'stupid' Sarah Palin was and how Obama was the only reasonable choice. Exit polls demonstrated a majority of union members knew no authentic facts about Sarah Palin but blindly voted for Obama *because they were told to.* In return, the unions expected Obama to push The Employee Free Choice Act through Congress that would give labor "organizers" the right to go into any business establishment and ask for a non-private vote by employees regarding whether they wanted to 'organize' or not. Bullying by organizers would become the rule of thumb so when the union added yet another establishment to their union roster the result would often be that the company would have to close its doors because it couldn't afford to stay in business any longer with the increased wage and benefit demands. Obama claims the economy is his number one focus but 'paying back' major supporters like the labor unions can only make the economy worse and showcases just how inexperienced and unready to lead Obama really is.

The day after his election Obama chose Illinois Rep. Rahm Emanuel as chief of staff. Emanuel is an orthodox Jew, which would seem to be in glaring contrast to the rabid anti-Israel stance of Obama's friend Rashid Khalidi. While that appointment sends mixed messages to the nation about the standpoint of the president-elect, only time will tell as Obama appears to not be supportive of Israel. Emanuel was President Clinton's senior policy advisor who is known for his 'hard nose' stand on issues.

President Clinton appointed Emanuel to the board of directors for 'Freddie Mac' in 2000 and during his short time there the agency was hit with numerous scandals regarding campaign contributions and accounting irregularities. That appointment is undoubtedly one Emanuel would like to down-play considering the collapse of the mortgage industry and the role 'Freddie Mac' and 'Fannie Mae' played in it. Emanuel was elected to the U.S. House of Representatives in 2002 where he remained until accepting president-elect Obama's offer of chief of staff. His hard-hitting combative political style allows Obama to be the 'good guy' because he can simply turn his 'pit bull' loose instead. Emanuel has an excellent reputation for getting things done, being a consummate fund-raiser, knowing all the political players, and knowing the ins and outs of Washington and the legislative process, traits that will greatly enhance Obama's ability to push his agenda through Congress.

Government is quickly taking control of the private economy, which increases public paranoia but Obama's objective in regard to gun restriction seems to have pushed the panic button for Americans who cherish the Second Amendment. Within the first week after the general election, guns were flying off the shelves and the trend continued in a clear and bold statement to government that citizens absolutely did not want government interfering with their rights under the Second Amendment but it was clear they feared Obama's intent once he took office. The message made it crystal clear that Americans do not intend to give up their guns and if government tries, it will surely face deadly opposition. Obama's legislative record proved him to be an ardent backer of gun control but fueling the fire of panic was Obama's choice of U.S. Attorney General. He chose Eric Holder who signed an amicus brief in 2008 supporting Washington, D.C.'s ban on the use of firearms of any sort for residential self-defense. He advocates federal licensing of handgun owners, rationing handgun sales to one a month, and imposing a three-day waiting period on gun sales. Former presidents such as George Washington himself clearly stated citizens should be armed because the day might come when they had to protect themselves against their own government and gun sales right after the election appear to prove Washington's point. The race to the far left by newly elected and appointed bureaucrats may very well be a precursor of things to come.

During the Clinton administration Democrats pushed legislation through Congress to force lending institutions to make even more loans to minorities or face discrimination penalties. Republicans didn't fight it because they saw it as "more loans, more money" for them. All through the Bush administration adjustable loans got millions of home buyers into homes with sub-prime loans by offering no money down and five years of low interest to be 'adjusted higher' at the five year mark. When that happened, millions of Americans could no longer pay their increased mortgages and homes went into foreclosure in droves. By the time the 2008 election rolled around the Democratic controlled Congress under the domination of Senate Majority Leader Harry Reid and House Speaker Nancy Pelosi was desperately trying to bail out the mortgage industry and cover their own greedy actions. By the end of Bush's administration Congress had an approval rating in the single digit – the lowest rating ever – so it wasn't surprising that the Congress tried to blame it all on Bush. Regardless, taxpayers were left to foot the bill for corporate greed and congressional lack of concern and another capitalistic venture was in danger of becoming nationalized, thus giving even more control to the federal government rather than less. The auto industry faced the same fate and Wall Street continued to meltdown as the economy entered a recession.

As president, Obama wants a 'Fairness Doctrine' pushed through Congress, which would essentially silence conservative radio talk show hosts like Rush Limbaugh and Sean Hannity. Liberals have little interest in promoting radio talk shows so conservative shows greatly outnumber them. In a cunning attempt to silence conservative talk shows, the so-called 'Fairness Doctrine' would require equal numbers of liberal and conservative talk shows. If few liberal shows are cultivated, conservative shows will be taken off the air until an equal amount of each exists, which is an astonishing tactic in attempting to silence those whose views one wishes to terminate. The directive would also require talk shows to provide equal amounts of time to both liberal and conservative viewpoints within any broadcast. Should the Congress pass the Fairness Doctrine, it is certain to be challenged on First

Amendment grounds but the mere attempt to censor free speech would cause a cloud of distrust to hang over the head of the Obama administration by freedom loving Americans. If the 'Fairness Doctrine' does not become an option to pursue, it would appear this president would not hesitate to use the FCC to bully stations and their sponsors in his quest to silence criticism as well as the conservative viewpoint.

Typical of the uneasiness felt during the campaign was Donna Stickler, a letter writer to the Las Vegas Review-Journal on October 23, 2008. She summed up the apprehension of many Americans when she wrote:

"Once upon a time, there was a charismatic and eloquent young leader who decided his nation needed a change, and that he was the one to implement it. The people were receptive and ready for change. He spoke passionately when denouncing the existing system, and the media loved him. Nobody questioned what he believed in or who his friends were. He would help the poor and bring free medical care and education to all. He would bring justice and equality. He said I am for hope and change, and I will bring you both. Few people bothered to ask about the change, and by the time the executioners' guns went silent, all personal firearms had been confiscated, along with most personal freedoms. When everyone was finally equal, they were (and are) equally poor, hungry and miserable. Their free education was (and is) all but worthless. Their free and universal health care was (and remains) a travesty. When the change was fully implemented, the country had been reduced to Third World status. More than a million people fled in small boats and rafts. The charismatic young leader was Fidel Castro; the nation is Cuba. The citizens of the United States would never fall for a charismatic, eloquent young leader who promises hope and change without asking, "What kind of change, and how much will it cost us?" ---- would we?"

America's world standing has been battered under the Bush administration so Obama will have a difficult task restoring America to the power and global influence it had prior to Bush's years in office. The nation's economic recession is the primary concern of citizens and a global economic meltdown, two wars, a festering nuclear crisis with Iran, on-going concern about new terrorist attacks on U.S. soil, and a renewed Al-Qaida resurgence in Afghanistan and Pakistan are among some of the overwhelming issues the new president inherits. He also intends to increase troop strength in Afghanistan, end the use of torture, and close the Guantanamo Bay prison in Cuba. Obama has stated the economic crisis will be his top priority and to that end he has appointed a disproportionate number of former Clinton administration staffers in the hope they can restore the economy to the health it enjoyed during Bill Clinton's administration. That will be a daunting task, however, since these are different times and different circumstances.

Those intending to rework the structure of democracy have warned that America would be taken over not by force, but by one small philosophical step at a time. Ezra Benson, President Eisenhower's Secretary of Agriculture, recalled a conversation he had with then-Soviet leader Nikita Kruschev during a tour of U.S. agricultural enterprises. Kruschev told Benson that U.S. citizens were being fed one small bite of Communism at a time and that eventually citizens would come to accept those ideals as the 'norm.' Mammoth out-of-control government would assist that endeavor and farther lead to a 'new world order' reality, which should concern voters when it comes to voting for a presidential candidate who espouses any anti-democracy rhetoric.

Professor Igor Panarin, leading Russian political analyst, professor at the Diplomatic Academy of the Russian Ministry of Foreign Affairs, and author of several information warfare books, had dire predictions for America's financial future in an interview published on November 24, 2008.[2] He said recent events have already started the financial collapse in the U.S. and could realistically result in *"a change in the regulatory system on a global financial scale where America will no longer be the world's financial regulator."* He observes that the dollar is not secured by anything, foreign debt has skyrocketed, and as short a time in the past as the 1980s there was no debt, yet the nation is currently trillions in debt.

He claims a pyramid like that can only collapse leaving China with its vast reserves and Russia as regulator in Eurasia as the global financial powers rather than the United States. Millions of U.S. citizens have lost their pensions and savings, inflation is at an all time high as is unemployment, and citizens are hugely dissatisfied with their life situation and angry at their ineffective government. That assertion was proven with the almost Pied Piper outcome of Obama's election. Many that believed in the 'change' promised by Obama have become disillusioned with his backtracking – even before taking the oath of office - on campaign promises he made. Millions of voters hoped Obama could work 'miracles' and make their lives much better but Panarin foresees tremendous disillusionment by late 2009 when it will become clear there are no 'miracles.'

Obama's early appointments reveal he is not as interested in improving ethics in government as he is in restructuring the nation's social policies as evidenced by his appointment of people dedicated to immensely expanding the scope of federal power. He plans an early push for socialized medicine, is eager to sign the Freedom of Choice Act on behalf of abortion options, has enlisted the advice of seven gays in his transition panel to help expand the rights of gay couples, and despite his campaign rhetoric to bring the troops home – has assembled known hawks who support the war, including Senator Clinton and Secretary of Defense Robert Gates on his foreign policy team and other key positions.

Appointments he has already made send a message that he is less concerned with baggage that may follow an appointee than pushing forward with a radical social agenda he avoided talking about during the campaign. His appointment of Carol Browner, former EPA advisor for the Clinton administration, as "special assistant to the President for energy and climate" is a case in point.[3] The position is a non-Cabinet post that does not require Senate confirmation, which means Ms. Browner will avoid scrutiny for her membership in the Commission for a Sustainable World Society, an off-shoot of Socialists International whose concepts support a radical agenda. By bestowing this appointment on Ms. Browner, Obama is circuitously endorsing her socialist agenda.

Much is unknown about the man that just became the 44th president or about his true intent for the country's direction so the nation has no other choice than to simply wait and watch as the *real* Barack Obama emerges.

Sir Winston Churchill once observed that, *"Past behavior is an indicator of future action."* That adage would appear to be especially timely with the 2008 election given the fact so much is unknown about the nation's new president. Throughout his campaign Obama touted 'change' ad nauseam, yet he never defined what HIS view of 'change' looked like. Voters simply inserted what THEY hoped 'change' would be but that left 'change' open to interpretation of each individual voter when the only analysis that mattered was the candidates and he left his meaning unknown and unexplained. His choice of Joe Biden as his running mate and early cabinet appointments soon after the general election pointed to good ole politics-as-usual Washington entrenched bureaucrats. Obama began surrounding himself with advisors and cabinet appointments that shared a Chicago connection or were formerly part of the Clinton administration. From long time Capitol Hill inhabitant Joe Biden, to numerous Clinton advisors, to Rahm Emanuel who was a senior advisor to Clinton, to Hillary Clinton as Secretary of State...Obama didn't seem to be bringing in 'new blood' to generate the 'change' he promised. It looks more like the Clinton administration revisited or a reunion of Chicago pals.

After disparaging the Bush administration and negatively tying John McCain to Bush throughout the campaign, Obama did an about face after the election by expressing support for many of Bush's decisions. That caused some radio and TV commentators to observe that Obama's administration may not result in significant 'change' after all. His administration will more than likely be a distinctly liberal one but perhaps any radical viewpoints he may have will be greatly softened by the shear reality of the office he now holds. He will be surrounded with all the history, pomp, and circumstance of old established

Washington, which is sure to have an affect on him. Despite the fear of many that he is too 'socialist' for the presidency, it is possible the 'change' may happen within Obama himself and he could become the ultimate 'traditional' leader. He is under tremendous pressure as the first black president to be exceptionally outstanding and set a precedent to prove a black man can be a dynamic leader. In the final analysis, a president has the ability to shape the office but the office could ultimately shape the president instead. Only time will tell.

One thing is certain, however. America has never faced a time like this since the administration of Abraham Lincoln. Recent events and philosophy have hugely divided the nation and what we are learning about the man who now occupies the Oval Office makes it clear we are a nation under siege and freedom could be the loser. While the character, policies, and presidency of Barack Hussein Obama is another book altogether, what is certain from this early appraisal is that we face an uncertain future that could either result in "we the people" taking back our country or in witnessing the "final chapter" of democracy.

REFERENCE

Chapter 8 - Presidential Overviews

1. U.S. Supreme Court Decision: 31 US (6 Pet.) 515 (1832); "*Worchester v. Georgia*" handed down by Justice John Marshall during the administration of Andrew Jackson.

2. Treaty of Guadalupe Hidalgo; 1838, National Archives.

3. www.en.wikipedia.org/wiki/Treaty_of_Guadalupe_Hidalgo

4. DiLorenzo, Thomas, *The Real Lincoln*, New York, Three Rivers Press, 2003, p. 59

5. Basler, Roy P., *The Collected Works of Abraham Lincoln*, Vol. III, p. 145-146; Fourth debate with Stephen A. Douglas at Charleston, Illinois on September 18, 1858. Lincoln stated he was "*not in favor of bringing about in any way the social and political equality of the white and black races.*"

6. DiLorenzo, Thomas, *The Real Lincoln*, New York, Three Rivers Press, 2003, p. 112-113

7. Livingston, Donald W., Emory University Philosopher, "*It was this spectacular lie that Lincoln embraced as his main rationale for denying the right of secession to the Southern states.*"

8. DiLorenzo, Thomas, *The Real Lincoln*, New York, Three Rivers Press, 2003, p. 102, 134-138

9. DiLorenzo, Thomas, *The Real Lincoln*, New York, Three Rivers Press, 2003, p. 119-122

10. Letter dated April 4, 1864 to editor of Frankfort Commonwealth, Albert G.Hodges of Kentucky.

11. Letter dated 1862 to New York Tribune Editor Horace Greeley

12. Letter to Treasury Secretary Salmon P. Chase. Lincoln admitted the proclamation was only a war measure and not an attempt at genuine emancipation.

13. U.S. Supreme Court case: 301 US 619 (1937)

14. Kessler, Ronald, *A Matter of Character*, New York, Sentinel/ Penguin Group, 2004, p. 107

15. Goodwin, Doris Kearns, *Lyndon Johnson and the American Dream*, St. Martin's Griffin, 1991, p. 203, 219, 314-317

16. Caro, Robert A., *The Years of Lyndon Johnson, Means of Ascent*, Borzoi Books, Published by Alfred A. Knopf, Inc., 1990, p. 181-191, 318-324, 328-330, 355, 362-363, 388-389, 393-394, 397-398

17. Goodwin, Doris Kearns, *Lyndon Johnson and the American Dream*, St. Martin's Griffin, 1991, p. 41, 241

18. Shane, Scott, New York Times, December 2, 2005, *Vietnam War Intelligence Deliberately Skewed, Secret Study Says*

19. Brinkley and Dyer, 2004, *American Presidency*

20. CNN, *The Reagan Years, the Iran Contra Scandal*, 2001

21. Witkin, Gordon, *The Nightmare of Idaho's Ruby Ridge*, September 11, 1995, U.S. News & World Report

22. Weaver, Randy, *Vicki, Sam, and America; How the Government Killed All Three*, Sunrise Publishing, 2003, p. 27-29

23. Gifford, Dan and Amy Sommer, *Waco: The Rules of Engagement*, 1997, Emmy award documentary film

24. Vidal, Gore, *The Meaning of Timothy McVeigh*, 2001, Vanity Fair

25. AP, *Bush Detainee Interrogation and Prosecution Plan Approved by Senate*, September 28, 2005, USA Today

26. Schlafly, Phyllis, *The NAFTA Super Highway*, August 23, 2006, Eagle Forum

27. Phillips, Kevin, *American Dynasty; Aristocracy, Fortune and the Politics of Deceit in the House of Bush*, Viking Press, 2004, p. Preface xi

28. Reuters, *Voters Unhappy With Bush and Congress*, October 17, 2007

29. Wilentz, Sean, Princeton University historian declared George W. Bush, *"one of the worst presidents in American history."* May 4, 2006, Rolling Stone magazine

Chapter 11 - New World Order

1. Buchanan, Patrick, *Where the Right Went Wrong*, 2004, New York, Thomas Dunne Books, an imprint of St. Martins Press

2. Grose, Peter, *Continuing the Inquiry: The Commission on Foreign Relations From 1921-1996*, New York: CFR: 1996, ISBN 0-876-09192-3

3. Hodgson, Godfrey, *Woodrow Wilson's Right Hand: The Life of Colonel Edward M. House*, 2006

4. http://en.wikipedia.org/wiki/League_of_Nations

5. Estulin, Daniel, *The Bilderberger Group*, Author's interview with Geoff Matthews, Nov-Dec 2005 issue of the Kingston (Canada) Eye Opener

6. Robbins, Alexandra, *Secrets of the Tomb: Skull and Bones, The Ivy League, and the Hidden Paths of Power*, 2003, Back Bay Books, ISBN 0-316-73561-2

7. Berkman, Gene, *The Trilateral Commission and the New World Order*, 1993, California, Renaissance Bookservice

8. Tancredo, Rep. Tom [R-Colo], *Halt the Security and Prosperity Partnership*, October 9, 2006, World Net Daily

9. Shaffer, Ralph and R. William Robinson, *Here Come the Thought Police*, November 11, 2007, Baltimore Sun

Chapter 13 - Executive Orders

1. Metcalf, Geoff, *Government Internment Camps: Recent Info on U.S. Concentration Camps*, May 11, 1998, World Net Daily

Chapter 17 - Military Commissions Act of 2006

1. Olbermann, Keith, *Beginning of the End of America*, MSNBC's 'Countdown with Keith Olbermann,' October 19, 2006, Re: Military Commissions Act of 2006: "*...a government more dangerous to our liberty, than is the enemy it claims to protect us from.*" "*Sadly, of course, the distance of history will recognize that the threat this generation of Americans needed to take seriously was you*" (George W. Bush).

2. Hamdan v. Rumsfeld, Superior Court Syllabus, p. 4, point 4

3. Ackerman, Bruce, Yale University professor of law and political science, interview with New York Times "*If Congress can strip courts of jurisdiction over cases because it fears their outcome, judicial independence is threatened.*"

Chapter 21 - 2008 Presidential Campaign Candidates

1. Pickler, Nedra, *Obama Debunks Claim About Islamic School*, January 24, 2007, Associated Press.

2. Fox News, *Obama and ACORN: Relationship May be More Extensive Than Candidate Says*, October 16, 2008

3. McCarthy, Andrew, *The L.A. Times Suppresses Obama's Khalidi Bash Tape*, October 27, 2008, National Review. McCarthy is an author and chair of the Foundation for the Defense of Democracies's Center for Law and Counterterrorism.

4. Jackson, David and McCormick, John, *Critics: Obama Endorsement Counters Calls For Clean Government*, June 12, 2007, Chicago Tribune.

5. Novak, Tim, *Eight Things You Need to Know About Obama and Rezko*, January 24, 2008, Chicago Sun-Times.

6. Hopkins, Kyle, *Joe the Plumber Was Once Joe the Alaskan*, October 24, 2008, Anchorage Daily News.

7. George Washington University, The Campaign Finance Institute, *Bipartisan Campaign Reform Act*.

8. Nowicki, Dan and Muller, Bill, *McCain Profile: The Keating Five*, March 01, 2007, Arizona Republic, Chapter VII: The Keating Five.

9. Holland, Megan, *Branchwater Will Investigate Monegan Case*, August 02, 2008, Anchorage Daily News.

Chapter 22 - America's Future

1. Arkansas Democrat-Gazette, *Interview of former Arkansas ACORN chair Dorothy Perkins*, September 3, 1987.

2. The Drudge Report, *Russian Analyst Predicts Decline and Breakup of USA*, November 25, 2008.

3. Dinan, Stephen, *Obama's Climate Czar Has Socialist Ties*, January 12, 2009, The Washington Post.

About the Author

Jessi Winchester ran for U.S. House of Representatives and Nevada Lieutenant Governor. A fed up citizen who fears for the future of the nation, her second book views each presidency through the lens of the Founders and the Constitution to help explain how we evolved from a Republic to the Socialist leaning crisis we face today. Email her at: jessiwinchester@att.net.

Printed in the United States
by Baker & Taylor Publisher Services